THE UK SLOW COOKER RECIPES BOOK

600+ Homemade Easy & Delicious Recipes for UK People

Author: Linda Olsen

TABLE OF CONTENTS

INTRODUCTION

United Kingdom foods You will need: can mean a lot to many people. Some people think about a rich dish with little spice, while others consider homemade meals from scratch that are overflowing with flavor. The genuine traditional UK food You will need: are a feast that speaks volumes on its own. It has a flavor that will be relished. Sauces and side dishes are intended to praise the fundamental course, not take the glory away from it, or mask its taste.

You can find all you want about UK foods You will need: in this eBook. You will be able to see amazing food You will need: you will love to make at home. If you are attempting to find truly United Kingdom food Recipes your smartest option will be to look at each of the You will need: in this eBook. This eBook has made the way for the information highway. You can look for the sorts of food You will need: you like in the UK, by the actual dish name. Any of these methods will lead you to an extensive list of English top picks that will melt in your heart, just as your mouth.

To make your cherished British food varieties at home, then, at that point, you will need to follow the measure of each recipe and methods for preparation. This will allow you to cook UK food varieties at home at whatever point you like.

This eBook is a five-star recipe eBook, why? because it will offer you a great and healthy breakfast, lunch, and dinner. There isn't anything more terrible than needing to taste your favorite dish and have it not been the thing you were anticipating.

At the point when you are preparing United Kingdom food, be ready to make most, if not all the meal, from scratch. These You will need: don't offer short routes utilizing processed, frozen, or canned foods. Every one of the food varieties ought to be new. This implies making batter using flour not a can of already made dough. Your sauces will likewise be produced using scratch, which will allow you to add spices and flavors depending on the need for them.

At the point when you are making British foods from scratch you will need to be sure to have sufficient time to prepare your meals. You should expect a somewhat longer time inputting your meal together. Everything will work out when you bring a little piece of London into your dining room for the night. Your family will thank you for investing some additional energy in dinner.

Whenever you have mastered the recipe, you will observe and find that preparing UK foods is simple not that tedious, and time-consuming. It is always a slow go at first, yet with time and experience, you will get faster with your meal preparation time. Allowing it to cook is the simple aspect.

600+ HOMEMADE EASY & DELICIOUS YOU WILL NEED: FOR UK PEOPLE

The familiar proverb that British food is boring and exhausting is an error and assuming you start to expose what's underneath, you'll find out many things to enjoy and appreciate. This eBook has assembled an amazing list of ***HOMEMADE EASY & DELICIOUS YOU WILL NEED: FOR UK PEOPLE***. It's a classic recipe you have to try - to kill the 'boring' myth for the last time. Since World War II, the British have been hampered with a reputation for grey, disheartening food, and a shortfall of culinary tradition.

This conviction, incited by the simple eating regimen of ration-book Britain, continues all around the world to the current day, but couldn't possibly be true. From all edges of the isles, Britain has countless delights and delicacies, all steeped with the traditions of the communities that give the nation its unique identity. Once you've worked your way through these amazing recipes you'll need to get out and explore the rest of what Britain brings to the table.

The You will need: in this eBook don't need a lot of equipment. Many of them are one-pot meals that just require a knife and slashing board, a spoon, and a medium pot. It merits putting resources into these simple pieces of cookery equipment as you will set aside loads of money assuming you can prepare your own food rather than depending on ready-prepared foods.

We trust this You will need: book will inspire you to make extraordinary tasting nourishment for you and your family and that this food will give a quality feast and build up great eating habits that will last them a lifetime.

1. Bubble and Squeak

PREPARATION TIME: 5 MINUTES SERVES 2

You will need:

- 1 onion, slashed
- Oil
- 1 cup cooked cabbage, spinach, or some other cooked green vegetables
- 2 cups pounded or hacked cook, bubbled or prepared potatoes
- Salt and pepper

Directions:

1. Lightly fry the onion in oil in a clean frying pan until delicate.
2. Include the green vegetables and fry for a few minutes. Season with salt and pepper.
3. Include the potatoes and form rissole shapes. Keep on broiling turning with a spatula each a few minutes, separating the blend so it is cooked everywhere and the potatoes begin to brown.

2. Cheeky Chicken Soup

PREPARATION TIME: 15 MINUTES SERVES 4

You will need:

- 1 chicken remains leftover from Sunday supper, ideally with a little meat on it
- 700ml of water
- 2 to 3 cups vegetables, such as onions, carrots, parsnip, leek
- 2 chicken stock cubes
- A dash soy sauce
- 1 teaspoon blended spices About 33% of a glass of wine, or even lager - whatever you have open
- 2 parcels of noodles or 2 small bunches of pasta stars

Directions:

1. Add chicken carcass into a clean pot.
2. Include water to totally cover the chicken, in addition to three inches
3. Sliced carrots, onions and some other vegetables, add to the pot and bring to the bubble.
4. Include the stock cubes, soy sauce, mixed herbs and wine or beer.
5. Turn down and simmer for about 20 minutes.
6. Gently remove the chicken carcass. In the event that there was meat on it, slice it off and add it to the soup
7. Add the noodles or pasta and stew for a further three minutes then, at that point, season and serve.

3. Roast Beef Stir Fry

PREPARATION TIME: 10 MINUTES SERVES 4

You will need:

- 1 tablespoon of oil
- 2 red peppers or yellow peppers, gently cut into strips
- 3 springs of onions, neatly sliced
- 50g of mushrooms, sliced
- 1 cup of leftover cooked green beans
- 150ml of beef stock
- 2 to 3 tablespoons of hoisin sauce
- 1 to 2 tablespoons of soy sauce
- 1 tablespoon of dry sherry
- 100–150g of leftover roast beef, gently thinly sliced
- 300g of medium whole-wheat noodles

Directions:

1. Heat the oil in a wok over high heat.
2. Include the peppers and onions and fry for two minutes.
3. Include the mushrooms and fry briefly.
4. Include the beans, stock, hoisin, soy, and sherry, and cook briefly.
5. Include the meat and throw well, keep on cooking for one more moment.
6. Include the noodles and cook for two additional minutes, or until everything is steaming hot.

4. Roast Cakes

PREPARATION TIME: 20 MINUTES SERVES 4

You will need:

- Leftover roast potatoes
- 2 eggs
- Leftover cooked vegetables like green beans, carrots, or broccoli, hacked into little pieces
- Breadcrumbs made from a stale baguette or loaf of bread
- Olive oil

Directions:

1. Separate the potatoes by crushing with a fork, however, leave some surface.
2. Add one egg and the vegetables and blend.
3. Beat the second egg in a different bowl.
4. Spread the breadcrumbs out onto a plate.
5. Take tablespoonfuls of the potato combination and shape them into round, level cakes.
6. Plunge everyone in the beaten egg, then, at that point, into the breadcrumbs and put away on a perfect plate.
7. Heat some oil in a clean skillet and fry the cakes on moderate hotness until crisp and golden, turning once. This should require around five minutes for each side.

5. Chicken Rissoles

PREPARATION TIME: 10 MINUTES SERVES 4

You will need:

- 1 onion, gently chopped
- 1 cup of leftover cooked chicken, gently chopped
- 2 eggs
- Breadcrumbs
- 1 apple, grated Salt & pepper Oil

Directions:

1. Fry the onion until brilliant then add the chicken and mood killer the hotness.
2. Beat the eggs, set to the side two tablespoons full, and blend the rest into the onion and chicken.
3. Save two tablespoons of breadcrumbs yet blend the rest, with the ground apple into the chicken and onion.
4. Shape into little cakes the size of a fishcake.
5. Plunge or dig them into the egg, then, at that point, the breadcrumbs before frying in oil until the two sides are browned. This requires around five minutes for every side, on moderate hotness.

6. Fajitas

PREPARATION TIME: 20 MINUTES SERVES 2

You will need:

- 1 red pepper cut into strips
- 1 red onion, finely slashed About
- 100g extra pork, destroyed
- 1 teaspoon smoked paprika Pinch of ground cumin
- 2 limes
- Olive oil
- Black pepper
- 4 little or 2 huge flour tortillas - you can freeze any additional ones
- 150ml regular yogurt
- 50g any hard cheddar, ground ¼ new red chilli, finely sliced
- 15 ready cherry tomatoes or 2 huge tomatoes, neatly sliced
- 1 little pack of new coriander, gently sliced
- Salt and pepper

Directions:

1. Blend the accompanying fixings in a huge bowl: pepper, onion, pork, paprika, cumin, juice of one lime, one teaspoon of olive oil, salt and pepper. Pass on this to marinade while you make the salsa.
2. Place the chilli, tomatoes, juice of one lime, coriander, salt, and pepper into a bowl and blend.
3. Set oil in a skillet on high hotness and pan-fried food vegetables and meat until cooked through around ten minutes.
4. Warm your tortillas individually in a dry skillet.

5. To gather, set the warmed tortillas on your serving plates, add the pork blend and salsa, sprinkle with cheddar, and roll up

7. Meat &Two Veg Biryani

PREPARATION TIME: 10 MINUTES SERVES 2

You will need:

- 100g basmati rice, cooked
- 1 egg, boiled (this is optional)
- 1 tablespoon of pure vegetable oil
- 1 small onion, gently chopped
- 1 clove garlic, sliced
- 1 tablespoon of curry paste
- Pinch of cinnamon
- ½ green or red chilli
- 3 clean curry leaves
- 1 portion of cooked leftover chicken
- Some bunch of vegetables, e.g., cauliflower, peppers, and green beans
- 100ml stock Half a lemon
- Salt & pepper to taste

Directions:

1. Heat the oil in a skillet or wok & delicately fry the onion & garlic until the onion is clear.
2. Include the curry glue, cinnamon, bean stew and curry leaves and mix for around two minutes. Include the meat and mix for ten minutes.
3. Include the vegetables and mix for a further a few minutes.
4. Delicately crease in the rice and blend through equally.
5. Include the stock, salt and pepper and let it stew for three to five minutes until most of the stock has vanished and the biryani is soggy.

6. Move to a plate, press over the lemon and topping with the cut bubbled egg.
7. Present with poppadoms and cucumber raita

8. Ragu for Pasta

PREPARATION TIME: 15 MINUTES SERVES 4

You will need:

- 2 tablespoons of original olive oil
- 2 carrots, gently sliced
- 2 onions, gently sliced
- 2 bowls of any leftover vegetables
- 2 - 4 leftover cooked sausages, gently sliced
- 4 ripe tomatoes, gently sliced
- 2 cups of vegetable stock
- 1 cup leftover red or white wine (optional)
- 1 tablespoon of tomato purée
- 2 to 4 tablespoons of milk Salt & pepper

Directions:

1. Heat the oil in a clean pan and add the carrots and onions. Sauté until delicate.
2. Mix in different vegetables and frankfurters.
3. Add the tomatoes, spices, and flavors.
4. Add the tomato purée, stock, and a portion of the wine (if utilizing), adding more as the sauce lessens.
5. Cover the ragu and stew on low hotness, blending every so often however long you can pause, somewhere around 60 minutes.
6. Mix in the milk towards the finish of cooking.

7. To serve, cook some pasta, scoop ragu on top and sprinkle with grated cheese.

9. Samosas

PREPARATION TIME: 25 MINUTES SERVES 4

You will need:

- 1.25kg of self-rising flour
- Cold water
- Sunflower oil
- Leftover cooked minced meat or leftover curry

Directions:

1. Make a ball of dough utilizing flour, two tablespoons of oil, and water.
2. Ply into a ball, then, at that point, make into around 15 little balls.
3. Utilize a moving pin to make everyone into a slender round flapjack the size of a saucer.
4. Channel the filling of any fluid and eliminate any huge flavors i.e., inlet leaves, cardamom cases.
5. Include a teaspoon of the filling to the focal point of every hotcake.
6. Wet the base edge of the hotcake by dunking your finger in water and seal the baked good. You can add an edging plan by bending the edge.
7. Fry in a skillet of profound cooking oil, or stick to broil sometime in the future

10. Tavas Lefkaritikos

PREPARATION TIME: 25 MINUTES SERVES 4

You will need:

- 500g leftover lamb, slice into cubes
- 1 onion, gently sliced
- 1 cup cooked rice
- 1 large potato, sliced
- 1 courgette, sliced
- 2 tomatoes, sliced
- 1 teaspoon of tomato purée
- ½ teaspoon of ground cumin
- Salt & pepper
- 1 tablespoon of olive oil

Directions:

1. Preheat the oven to 160°C
2. In an earthen pot, place a layer of meat, a layer of rice, onion, potato, and courgette, seasoning each layer with salt & pepper.
3. Wrap up by placing the tomatoes on top.
4. Break up the tomato purée in a little high temp water, add the cumin and olive oil and pour over the top.
5. Put sufficient water in the pot to cover the food and spot it on the stove for around two hours.

11. Fishcakes

PREPARATION TIME: 30 MINUTES SERVES 4

You will need:

- 400g of cooked potatoes, crushed
- 200g of cooked fish, skin & bones eliminated
- 2 spring onions, finely cleaved
- 1 small bunch new coriander, gently sliced
- 1 teaspoon of stew pieces
- 4 tablespoons of dry breadcrumbs
- 1 egg, beaten Sunflower oil, for cooking
- Salt &dark pepper

Directions:

1. Chip the fish into little pieces.
2. In a bowl, add the crushed potatoes, fish, spring onions, coriander, and stew drops.
3. Shape the blend into eight fishcakes around 1cm thick.
4. Dip each one in the beaten egg and coat with the breadcrumbs
5. Refrigerate for about 20 minutes.
6. Heat one tablespoon of oil in a container and cook the fishcakes on moderate hotness for 5 minutes on each side

12. Fish Salad

PREPARATION TIME: 10 MINUTES SERVES 2

You will need:

- Any leftover cooked fish (all bones must be removed)
- 2 boiled or baked potatoes, slice into chunks
- 1 boiled egg, gently sliced
- ¼ of a salad leaf
- 1 small sliced cooked beetroot
- 1 can of sweetcorn
- 2 teaspoons of sunflower seeds
- Salt & pepper Mayonnaise

Directions:

1. Flake the fish and slice other ingredients.
2. Toast the seeds in a dry griddle until it turns golden
3. Cautiously combine the salad ingredients all together, at that point, sprinkle the seeds on top.
4. Dress with homemade or bought salad dressing.

13. Fish Soup

PREPARATION TIME: 15 MINUTES SERVES 4

You will need:

- 1 stick celery
- 2 clean onions
- 2 cups of vegetables (carrot, parsnip, leek, tomato)
- 320g leftover of white fish
- 1 teaspoon of dried herbs
- Salt & pepper
- 3 tablespoons of olive oil
- 1 cup of rice

Directions:

1. Wash and chop the vegetables as a whole and spot them in a pan or skillet.
2. Next cover the vegetables with water until it arrives at two creeps above them.
3. Heat up the vegetables with the rice, spices, salt, pepper & oil.
4. At the point when the vegetables are practically or almost ready, add the extra fish. Heat through and switch off the heat.

14. Fish Quiche

PREPARATION TIME: 60 MINUTES SERVES 8

You will need:

- 200g of original plain flour
- 100g of salted butter
- 1 egg, slightly beaten
- 3 eggs and 225ml of milk
- 150g of any hard cheese, grated
- 200g of any leftover cooked fish (all skin and bones must be removed)
- Add Cherry tomatoes, 2 peppers or any leftover cooked fish & vegetables
- Salt and pepper

Directions:

1. Rub together the flour and spread until the blend looks like fine breadcrumbs.
2. Add the egg a little at a time until the blend shapes a batter. Envelop by stick film and leave in the ice chest for 30 minutes prior to utilizing.
3. Carry out the baked good on a softly floured surface and use it to line a flan dish or tart tin. Delicately press into shape and trim away the abundance with a blade. Chill for 20 minutes.
4. Cover the cake with baking paper, load up with earthenware baking beans (or dry rice or beans saved for the reason), and prepare at 190oC (gas

mark 5) for 15 minutes. Eliminate baking paper and beans and pass them on to cool.

5. Presently beat together the eggs, milk, and cheddar and season with salt and pepper. Empty blend into cake shell. Add your preferred extra fish and vegetables. Prepare at 180oC (gas mark 4) for around 30 minutes until the quiche is simply firm and brilliant.

15. Veggie Burgers

PREPARATION TIME: 20 MINUTES SERVES 6

You will need:

- 3 slices of bread, make into breadcrumbs
- 1 onion, sliced
- 1 garlic of clove, crushed
- 1 tablespoon of original oil
- 2 tablespoons pure flour Herbs
- Salt & pepper to be added
- 1 egg
- 1 cup leftover vegetables, such as carrot, peas or sweetcorn. You could also include baked beans

Directions:

1. Combine every one of the You will need: as one aside from the flour and oil, mashing the beans with your hands while blending and forming into balls the size of an egg.
2. Set the flour on a plate. Cover the balls with a meager layer of flour and afterward make a leveled burger shape.
3. The burgers can be baked or fried. If frying, place oil in a skillet or pan under moderate hotness and cook the burgers for around five minutes on

each side. If baking, preheat the broiler to 200°C (gas mark 6), put it on a plate with a shower of oil, and heat for 15 - 20 minutes

16. Daddy's Heart-Filling Potato Dish

PREPARATION TIME: 10 MINUTES SERVES 2

You will need:

- Boiled potatoes
- 3 tablespoons of pure vegetable oil
- 2 teaspoons of mustard seeds
- 1 teaspoon of salt
- ½ teaspoon of halide (yellow powder)
- ½ teaspoon of chilli powder

Directions:

1. Mash boiled potatoes
2. Heat the vegetable oil in a frying pan
3. Add the mustard seeds and allow them to pop!
4. At the point when they complete the process of popping, add the potatoes to the pan alongside the salt, halide, and chilli powder
5. Add the lemon juice and vinegar.
6. Blend well & serve.

17. Potato Pancakes

PREPARATION TIME: 15 MINUTES SERVES 4

You will need:

- 250g leftover mashed potatoes
- 1 egg or 2 eggs
- 2 tablespoons of self-rising flour
- 100ml milk or water
- 1 teaspoon of pure baking powder
- Vegetable oil Optional

Directions:

1. Blend all You will need: (aside from the oil) together to make a batter.
2. Heat the oil in a clean pan.
3. Drop tablespoonfuls of the player into the frying pan.
4. Fry until the highest point of the latkes shows up firm and afterward turn over and fry the opposite side until brown.
5. Enjoy your meal

18. Potato Salad

PREPARATION TIME: 10 MINUTES SERVES 2

You will need:

- 3 potatoes (it's all depends on the amount you have)
- 2 spring of onions, finely sliced Salad cream
- 1 teaspoon of pure olive oil
- Black pepper & vegetable stock powder for seasoning

Directions:

1. Scrub the potatoes making a point to leave the skins on. Cut them into even pieces.
2. Bubble for 20 minutes or until delicate and pass on to cool.
3. In a huge bowl, combine every one of the fixings as one.
4. Taste and add more plate of mixed greens cream or prepare if necessary.

19. Guacamole

PREPARATION TIME: 15 MINUTES SERVES 2

You will need:

- 1 or 2 ripe of avocadoes
- 1 juice of lemon
- 1 clean of garlic clove, crushed
- 2 tomatoes, peeled & chopped
- ½ onion (red or white), finely chopped
- 2 tablespoons finely chopped celery (optional)
- 2 tablespoons of finely chopped parsley
- 2 tablespoons of pre olive oil Salt & pepper

Directions:

1. Peel & squeeze the avocadoes lightly with a clean wooden spoon.
2. Include lemon juice, garlic, tomatoes, onion & celery.
3. Stir all in the parsley or coriander, pure olive oil, salt & pepper.

20. Hot Chickpea Salad

PREPARATION TIME: 15 MINUTES SERVES 2

You will need:

- 2 tablespoons of pure olive oil
- 2 cloves garlic, gently crushed
- 1 small red chilli
- 2 bowls of leftover vegetables e.g., spring onions, peppers, green beans, spinach, chard
- 400g of chickpeas
- Fresh tarragon Juice of 2 limes
- Salt & pepper

Directions:

1. In a clean frying pan, heat the olive oil over medium hotness and afterward add the garlic and bean stew and mix.
2. Include the vegetables and cook until they are mellowed yet at the same time have a nibble. Vegetables that take more time to cook might be added first.
3. Add the chickpeas and tarragon leaves and permit the blend to cook delicately for five minutes or until the chickpeas are hot.

4. Pour the lime juice over the blend and mix. Season and permit it to rise for a couple of moments until the fluid has reduced.

21. Onion Bhajis

PREPARATION TIME: 35 MINUTES SERVES 4

You will need:

- 4 medium potatoes, gently peeled & quartered
- 2 onions, peeled & thinly sliced
- A handful of chopped spinach, carrot or cauliflower, whichever you have
- 1 to 2 green chillies, gently sliced
- 1 handful of fresh coriander leaves, sliced
- 2 teaspoons of garam masala
- ½ teaspoon of pure turmeric
- 1 lemon, juice only
- 1 teaspoon of pure baking powder
- 250g of pure flour
- 3 tablespoons of undiluted rice flour (optional)
- Pure sunflower oil for cooking

Directions:

1. Meagerly cut the bits of potato and blend in a bowl with the onion cuts, hacked vegetables, bean stew, coriander, and flavors.

2. Mix in the baking powder, rice flour, and enough gram flour with the goal that the vegetables are covered.
3. Mix in the lemon juice and enough water to make a thick player that covers the vegetables. Heat one cup of oil in a skillet. Cautiously add one tablespoon of the blend for each bhaji and cook for around five minutes.
4. Turn part of the way through cooking with the goal that they are brilliant brown on the two sides.
5. Gently remove from the frying pan with an opened spoon and channel on kitchen paper to eliminate excess oil.

22. Super Veggie Strudel

PREPARATION TIME: 30 MINUTES SERVES 8

You will need:

- 1 onion, finely sliced
- 2 cloves of garlic, finely sliced
- Olive oil
- 2 to 3 cups chopped vegetables
- Salt & pepper
- Fresh parsley or any other herbs you have, finely chopped
- 150g of cheddar
- 500g block of puff pastry

Directions:

1. Fry the onion and garlic in some pure olive oil.
2. Include the vegetables and fry until half-cooked.
3. Channel off any fluid and afterward add salt and pepper, spices, and cheddar.
4. Blend well.
5. Preheat the broiler to 190°C

6. Carry out the baked good to about ½ cm thick and lay it with the goal that it is half-covering a baking plate.
7. Put the filling on the baked good, as an afterthought that covers the baking plate.
8. Cover the loading up with the excess portion of the baked good and seal the edges.
9. Puncture the highest point of the strudel with a fork and coat with some olive oil or beaten egg.
10. Heat in the oven for 45 minutes

23. Tomato Sauce

PREPARATION TIME: 15 MINUTES SERVES 4

You will need:

- 2 tablespoons of pure olive oil
- 1 onion
- 1 garlic clove, crushed
- 1 stick celery, gently sliced
- 2 to 3 cups of vegetables
- 1 teaspoon of original brown sugar
- 1 teaspoon of balsamic vinegar
- 400g can plum tomatoes
- 1 teaspoon of fresh or dried thyme
- Salt & pepper

Directions:

1. Heat the oil in a dish.
2. Include the onion, garlic, and celery and cook until mellowed, around five minutes.

3. Include the leftover vegetables, and proceed with cooking for five minutes, blending infrequently.
4. Include the earthy-colored sugar, balsamic vinegar, tomatoes, and spices and bring to the bubble.
5. Season, decrease the hotness, and stew for 15 minutes.
6. Cautiously mix the sauce with a hand blender.

24. Vegetable Patties

PREPARATION TIME: 25 MINUTES SERVES 4

You will need:

- 450g of pure plain flour
- 150g of butter
- 1 teaspoon of undiluted turmeric
- 1 teaspoon of pure curry powder
- 1 onion, gently sliced
- 1 teaspoon of minced garlic
- 2 teaspoons of minced ginger
- 3 handfuls peas, sweetcorn, shredded cabbage
- ½ scotch bonnet pepper, gently sliced
- 2 tablespoons of white vinegar
- 1 teaspoon of thyme leaves
- 200ml of vegetable or chicken stock
- 1 handful of dry breadcrumbs
- 1 egg, beaten
- Salt & black pepper

- Pure of sunflower oil for cooking

Directions:

1. Filter together the flour, turmeric, and curry powder in a bowl. Focus on the margarine utilizing your fingertips until brittle.
2. Gradually mix insufficient virus water to make a mixture and afterward wrap and refrigerate.
3. Heat one tablespoon of oil in a skillet and cook the onion, garlic, scotch cap, and ginger for a couple of moments.
4. Mix in the thyme leaves and vegetables and cook for five minutes.
5. Add the stock, white vinegar salt, and pepper. Bring to the bubble and afterward stew for 15 minutes. Assuming that the blend turns out to be too dry add a little water.
6. Mix in the breadcrumbs and eliminate the hotness.
7. Preheat the broiler to 200°C (gas mark 6) and oil a baking plate with oil or margarine.
8. Partition the baked good into balls and carry out into circles around 15cm across. Brush the external edge of the baked good with egg then, at that point, place one tablespoon of filling aside. Overlap the baked good into equal parts and delicately seal down the edges utilizing a fork.
9. Put the patties on the baking plate, brush with the beaten egg, and heat for 20-25 minutes until golden.

25. Vegetable Soup

PREPARATION TIME: 20 MINUTES SERVES 2

You will need:

- 30g of butter
- 2 sticks celery
- 2 broccoli stalks and some florets
- 2 carrots Any other vegetables you have in the fridge
- 1 onion
- 1 clove garlic
- 2 tablespoons of leftover cooked potato
- 1 teaspoon of mixed dried herbs
- 1 chicken or vegetable stock cube
- 600ml of water
- 2 tablespoons of plain yoghurt or coconut milk
- Salt & pepper

Directions:

1. Cut every one of the vegetables into pieces.

2. Put each of the fixings aside from the yogurt/coconut milk into a skillet and bring to the bubble.
3. Go down to a stew and pass on to cook for 30-45 minutes, blending once in a while.
4. Switch off the hotness and permit it to cool for five minutes.
5. Fill a blender and mix until smooth (assuming excessively thick, add more water).
6. Season and mix in the yogurt or coconut milk.
7. Re-heat if essential however don't boil.

26. Spicy Herb Paste

PREPARATION TIME: 30 MINUTES SERVES 4

You will need:

- 1 small onion
- 2cm piece of ginger
- 3 garlic cloves
- 2 lemongrass stalks
- 25g fresh red or green chillies
- 75g coriander leaves, stalks & roots
- 1 tablespoon of coriander seeds
- 1 tablespoon of salt
- 1 teaspoon of turmeric
- 2 tablespoons of honey
- Juice of a lemon
- 2 tablespoons of pure sunflower oil

Directions:

1. Peel and trim onion, ginger, garlic, lemongrass, chilies, and new coriander, depending on the situation.
2. Toast coriander seeds on low hotness in a little dry griddle for a couple of moments until a shade is hazier and smell fragrant.
3. Place all fixings aside from sunflower oil in a food processor. Beat it to separate the fixings, then, at that point, a process for somewhere around a moment to accomplish a practically smooth glue. Presently leisurely add the oil while handling some more.
4. At the point when you're prepared to utilize the glue, fry for a couple of moments to bring some relief from the crude shallot and garlic, then, at that point, add chicken stock or coconut milk and whatever vegetables or extra meat you have for a speedy and simple soup or curry.
5. Serve with noodles or rice.

27. Quesadillas

PREPARATION TIME: 10 MINUTES SERVES 4

You will need:

- 8 flour tortilla wraps
- 150g of grated cheese
- 100g of mushrooms
- 2 peppers or any leftover cooked vegetables
- Salt & pepper

Directions:

1. Place one of the tortillas into an enormous griddle and dry fry it over medium hotness.
2. Layer the vegetables and cheddar onto the tortilla and put another on top. Season to taste.
3. Allow the tortilla to cook on each side until toasted.
4. Rehash with the excess fixings
5. Cut the quesadillas into cuts like a pizza.

28. Pumpkin gnocchi with pumpkin sauce

You will need:

For the gnocchi:

- 1kg of pumpkin
- 2 potatoes
- 400 to 500g of pure potato flour
- 1 teaspoon of salt
- ½ teaspoon of ground nutmeg

For the sauce:

- 1 tablespoon of pure olive oil
- 1kg of pumpkin
- 4 tomatoes
- 200g of spinach, sliced
- 3 cloves garlic, finely chopped
- 4 pure of sprigs rosemary
- 500ml of water
- 1 vegetable stock cube

- 1 red chilli
- Salt & pepper

Directions:

1. Set the oven to 200oC. Put the potatoes in the broiler to heat until delicate. This should require 60 minutes.
2. Cut the pumpkin into equal parts or quarters, scoop out the seeds, brush with olive oil, and heat for ½ an hour until delicate.
3. Scoop out the tissue of the pumpkin and the potato. Presently either pound it with a fork, or with a potato ricer, or put it in a food processor until extremely smooth.
4. Join all the gnocchi fixings with a spatula. The blend ought to be tacky however remain together when moved in a ball. Add some more flour if essential.
5. Partition into tablespoon-size balls and roll these into 2cm hotdogs on a floured surface. Cut the butter into 1cm pieces and turn over a fork to leave edges.
6. Place the gnocchi onto a floured baking plate until required and presently set up the sauce. Slash the pumpkin tissue into 1cm pieces.
7. Heat the oil in a weighty lined enormous skillet and add every one of the fixings separated from the spinach. Put the top on and leave for 25 minutes on low hotness.
8. At the point when the pumpkin is delicate mood killer the hotness, mix in the spinach and cover.
9. Presently cook the gnocchi: Bring a skillet of salted water to the bubble and drop about 33% of the gnocchi into the dish. Cook for a couple of moments until they ascend to the top and afterward fill a colander and present with the pumpkin sauce.

29. Pumpkin pie

PREPARATION TIME: 40 MINUTES SERVES 12

You will need:

For the pastry:

- 200g of pure flour
- 100g of unsalted butter
- 25g ground almond
- 25g icing sugar
- 1 egg, lightly beaten

For the filling:

- 750g of pumpkin, seeds removed & cut into 2cm sized cubes
- 140g of caster sugar
- ½ tablespoon of salt
- ½ tablespoon of nutmeg
- ½ tablespoon of cinnamon
- 2 eggs, beaten
- 25g of butter, lightly melted
- 175g of pure milk

Directions:

1. Rub together the flour and butter until the blend takes after fine breadcrumbs.
2. Include the ground almond, icing sugar, and egg and blend until it shapes a batter.
3. Envelop by stick film and leave in the cooler for thirty minutes prior to utilizing.
4. Carry out the baked good on a daintily floured surface and use it to line a flan dish or tart tin. Delicately press into shape and trim away the overabundance with a blade. Chill for 20 minutes.
5. Cover the baked good with baking paper, load up with earthenware baking beans, and heat at 190oC for 15 minutes. Eliminate baking paper and beans and cook for an additional ten minutes then, at that point, eliminate and pass on to cool.
6. Now place the pumpkin in a skillet, cover it with water and bring it to the bubble. Cover and stew for 14 minutes until delicate.
7. Channel the pumpkin in a sifter however at that point put the strainer over a bowl and push the pumpkin through so you have a mash.
8. Turn the broiler on to 220oC (gas mark 7) and presently include the wide range of various filling fixings to the pumpkin and consolidate. Empty the filling blend into the cake case and heat for ten minutes.
9. Now turn the broiler down to 180oC (gas mark 4) and prepare for a further 35 - 40 minutes. Allow cooling before eating.

30. Pumpkin and coconut curry

PREPARATION TIME: 45 MINUTES SERVES 4

You will need:

- ½ tablespoon of pure olive oil
- 2 tablespoons of Thai red curry paste
- 1 white onion, sliced
- 2 stalks of clean lemongrass, outer husk removed & sliced
- ½ teaspoon of cardamom seeds
- ½ tablespoon of mustard seeds
- 750g pumpkin, seeds must be removed & sliced into chunks
- 125ml of vegetable stock
- 200ml of pure coconut milk
- 200g of can chickpeas
- 2 clean limes
- 14g of fresh coriander, sliced
- Salt & pepper

Directions:

1. Heat the oil in a sauté skillet, include the curry glue, onions, lemongrass, cardamom, and mustard seeds, and delicately fry for a few minutes until fragrant.
2. Include the pumpkin into the skillet and mix to cover in the glue.

3. Pour in the stock and coconut milk and bring to a stew.
4. Include the chickpeas and cook for 10 - 15 minutes until the pumpkin is delicate. Season to taste.
5. Squeeze the juice of one lime into the curry and cut the excess lime into wedges.

31. Pumpkin, kale and lentil salad

PREPARATION TIME: 15 MINUTES SERVES 4

You will need:

- 600g of pure pumpkin, seeds must be removed sliced into pieces about 3cm thick
- Pure olive oil, for drizzling
- ½ teaspoon of chilli flakes
- 1 teaspoon of ground cumin
- 1 teaspoon of ground coriander
- 150g of sliced kale
- 1 garlic clove, sliced
- Seeds of ½ of pomegranate
- 100g of puy lentils (dark black lentils)
- 1 tablespoon of tahini
- 1 tablespoon of pure olive oil
- 2 teaspoon of tamari soy sauce
- 1 lime of juice
- 1 tablespoon of clean water
- Salt & pepper

Directions:

1. Preheat the oven to 180oC (gas mark 4).

2. Cut off the top and lower part of the pumpkin. Slice it down the middle, eliminate the seeds, and cut it into 3cm 3D shapes.
3. Place the pumpkin in a huge blending bowl, shower with olive oil, and include the flavors, salt, and pepper. Blend well and lay the pumpkin 3D squares on a baking plate.
4. Broil in the stove for 30 - 40 minutes. The pumpkin is prepared when the skin is soft, it has some tone, and is soft the whole way through when pricked with a knife.
5. Meanwhile, flush the lentils in chilly water, include to a container, cover with water and bring to the bubble. Season and stew until delicate; around 20 minutes to cook. Channel and pass on to cool.
6. Make the tahini dressing by whisking the tahini and lime squeeze together. Include the water to the bowl progressively and blend to shape a smoother glue and rehash until the combination has the consistency of twofold cream. Include the tamari and olive oil and blend again until you have a smooth pourable consistency.
7. Include the kale in a blending bowl, pour over the dressing and blend manually. This will marinate and mellow the kale.
8. Put the kale on a serving platter, disperse the lentils and afterward top with the boiled pumpkin. Include the pomegranate seeds, salt, pepper, and shower with olive oil to serve.

32. Leftover spaghetti cake

PREPARATION TIME: 20 MINUTES SERVES 4

You will need:

- 2 eggs
- Pinch cayenne pepper
- Salt & pepper
- Grated cheese
- A carrot or courgette, grated
- Leftover cooked spaghetti in sauce
- 2 tomatoes, gently sliced

Directions:

1. In a large bowl, crack the eggs together.
2. Season with cayenne, salt, and pepper. Include the carrot or courgette.
3. Include a large portion of the cheddar.
4. Include the spaghetti and sauce and combine them as one.
5. Preheat the broiler to 200°C
6. Line a cake tin with baking foil and solidly press the blend into the tin.
7. Top with cut tomato and the excess cheddar.
8. Overlap the baking foil over the highest point of the cake.
9. Prepare for 30 minutes. Allow cooling before cutting as a delicious lunch

33. Minestrone soup

PREPARATION TIME: 20 MINUTES SERVES 2

You will need:

- 1 onion, sliced
- ½ a fresh chilli, sliced
- 2 cloves garlic, sliced
- Pure olive oil
- 4 cups of sliced vegetables such as carrots, potatoes, or kale
- 1 teaspoon of balsamic vinegar
- 1 tin sliced tomato
- 1 cup of hot water with a stock cube diluted in it
- 2 tablespoons of tomato purée
- Salt & pepper
- 2 cups of cooked pasta
- 1 teaspoon of pure herbs

Directions:

1. In an enormous pot sauté the onion, chilli, and garlic in the olive oil.
2. Include the vegetables and cook for around five minutes, blending oftentimes.
3. Include the balsamic vinegar and mix for a further two minutes. Include the tomatoes and stock and afterward permit to stew until the vegetables are cooked.

4. Mix in the tomato purée, salt, and pepper. Include the pasta.
5. Include sufficient water to cover and take back to the bubble. In the case of utilizing cooked pasta, just cook until warmed. In the case of using dried pasta, stew for five to ten minutes until cooked.
6. Spoon into bowls and present with a little grated cheese on top.

34. Pasta frittata

PREPARATION TIME: 20 MINUTES SERVES 2

You will need:

- Leftover cooked pasta
- Eggs - 1 for every100g of pasta
- Salt & pepper
- Chilli
- Grated cheese
- Leftover cooked vegetables or meat, sliced into pieces
- Pure oil

Directions:

1. Crack the eggs in a clean bowl.
2. Include salt, pepper, stew, and cheddar.
3. Include the vegetables.
4. Include the pasta in the bowl and blend well.
5. For some oil in a skillet (ideally one with a metal handle) and furthermore set the barbecue on simultaneously.
6. Empty the entire mixture into the skillet and cook for 2 minutes on high heat.
7. Remove the hob and barbecue until brown and fresh on top

35. Pasta salad

PREPARATION TIME: 30 MINUTES SERVES 4

You will need:

- Small bunch fresh parsley
- 400g of leftover pasta
- 2 springs of onions
- 350g cut pitted olives
- 250g of cherry tomatoes
- 2 cans of tuna in water (240g)
- Grated parmesan cheese
- Mozzarella cheese
- 4 tablespoons of green pesto
- 2 tablespoons of mayonnaise
- Salt & pepper
- Pure olive oil

Directions:

1. Slice the parsley, spring onions, and cherry tomatoes and cut the mozzarella into pieces.
2. Add in a bowl with the extra pasta, fish, olives, and parmesan.
3. Blend in the green pesto and mayonnaise.

4. Include salt, pepper, and oil to preferred taste.

36. Bits and pieces omelette

You will need:

- Mixed salad leaves
- Pure olive oil
- 4 eggs
- 250ml of undiluted milk
- 2 teaspoons of pesto
- Cooked couscous
- Feta cheese

Directions:

1. Slice the leaves and put in a frying bot with some oil and cook tenderly to wither.
2. Whisk the egg with the milk and pesto in a container.
3. Include the couscous to the griddle.
4. Pour the egg combination onto the couscous and mix delicately
5. Sprinkle the cheddar on top.
6. Cook on the hob for ten minutes over a medium hotness.
7. Move to the barbecue and cook the top for five minutes.
8. Remove from the barbecue and pass on to represent five minutes.
9. Delicately release edges and turn out onto a plate

37. Ginger and cashew fried rice

PREPARATION TIME: 10 MINUTES SERVES 2

You will need:

- 1 onion, sliced
- Small mushrooms
- 1 clove of garlic, sliced
- Small knob of ginger, sliced
- Pure oil
- 2 handfuls of cashew nuts
- 2 cups of cooked leftover rice
- 1 tablespoon of dark soy sauce
- Salt & pepper

Directions:

1. Fry the onion, mushrooms, garlic, and ginger in the oil.
2. Include the cashew nuts.
3. Include the rice and soy sauce and mix until very much blended and the rice is covered by the oil.
4. Include a tablespoon of water, cover, and steam briefly.
5. Season & serve.

38. Couscous fritters

PREPARATION TIME: 30 MINUTES SERVES 4

You will need:

- 1 cup of cooked millet
- 1 onion, sliced
- 2 cloves of garlic, sliced
- ¼ cup of pure olives, sliced
- 1 tablespoon of peanut butter
- Dried herbs
- You can also add any leftover vegetables
- Salt & pepper
- Pure sunflower oil
- 1 egg
- Breadcrumbs for coating

Directions:

1. In a clean bowl, mix every one of the above You will need: aside from the oil, egg, and breadcrumbs, then, at that point, shape into little rissoles.
2. Whisk the egg in a bowl and plunge the squanders in, prior to covering in breadcrumbs.

3. Heat the oil in a frying bot & fry the fritters for a couple of moments on each side.

39. Stir fried rice

PREPARATION TIME: 10 MINUTES SERVES 2

You will need:

- Pure vegetable oil
- 1 onion, sliced
- 2 cloves of garlic, sliced
- 1 fresh chilli, sliced
- 2 cups of cooked rice
- Any vegetables (red pepper, cabbage, mushrooms)
- 2 tablespoons of soy sauce or tamari

Directions:

1. Heat the oil in a frying pot, include the onion, and cook until mellowed.
2. Include the garlic and stew and cook for a couple of moments.
3. Include the rice and mix until covered and warmed through.
4. Include the cooked vegetables
5. At the point when the vegetables are warmed through, include a few tablespoons of soy sauce, mix and serve.

40. Stuffed peppers

PREPARATION TIME: 25 MINUTES SERVES 4

You will need:

- 4 to 5 peppers
- 50g of feta cheese
- 50g of hard cheese, such as cheddar
- 50g of roquefort cheese
- Salt & pepper
- 1 cup cooked leftover rice
- Mint ½ small chilli, sliced
- 2 cloves of garlic, sliced
- ½ cup of pure oil
- ½ cup of wine
- 1 teaspoon of oregano

Directions:

1. Wash the peppers and afterward open one side with a blade, eliminating the seeds.

2. Grind the cheddar and blend in a bowl with salt, pepper, rice, mint, stew, and garlic.
3. Fill the peppers with the cheddar/rice blend and put them in a baking dish.
4. Blend the oil in with the wine, salt, pepper, and oregano, and pour this combination over the peppers.
5. Cover with foil and prepare for 45 minutes at 180°C

41. Three tin curries

PREPARATION TIME: 5 MINUTES SERVES 3

You will need:

- 2-3 tablespoons of pre sunflower oil
- 1 teaspoon of black mustard seeds
- 1 teaspoon of cumin seeds
- 400ml of pure coconut milk
- 1 teaspoon of salt
- 1 teaspoon of pure mild red chilli powder
- 2 teaspoons of ground cumin
- ½ teaspoon of pure turmeric powder
- 400g of tin chickpeas, must be drained
- 415g of tin baked beans
- Pure juice of half a lemon
- 2 to 3 coriander sprigs, sliced

Directions:

1. Heat oil on low hotness in an enormous dish. Include mustard and cumin seeds and let them sizzle and fly for a couple of moments, then, at that point, include coconut milk. Accept care as it might splutter.
2. Include salt, chilli powder, cumin, and turmeric, and mix to combine. In the case of utilizing, include garlic, ginger, and cover and stew for ten minutes.
3. Now include the chickpeas, baked beans, and any extra vegetables.
4. Mix well, cover, and pass on to stew for around five minutes until everything is totally warmed.
5. At long last mix in lemon juice and new coriander and present with anything you have - rice, couscous, a thick cut of toast, pitta bread, or naan bread.

42. Croutons

PREPARATION TIME: 15 MINUTES SERVES 4

You will need:

- Slightly stale bread
- Pure olive oil
- Salt & pepper
- Optional: Dried or fresh herbs, e.g., thyme, oregano, dill or rosemary Chilli flakes or other spices
- Garlic, neatly sliced

Directions:

1. Before bread is too difficult to even consider cutting, cut or tearing it into crouton-sized pieces. In a bowl throw the cube of bread in a decent shower of oil, salt, pepper, and spices, flavors, or garlic (if utilizing).
2. Heat a frying pot, add the bread and fry over medium hotness for a couple of moments, throwing often, until the bread is fresh and beginning to shade.

3. Then again, spread the bread over a baking plate and prepare at 180°C (gas mark 4) for around ten minutes, throwing partially through.
4. Spread the bread garnishes over a plate fixed with kitchen paper to cool totally, then, at that point, store in an air-tight container.

43. Panzanella

PREPARATION TIME: 20 MINUTES SERVES 2

You will need:

- 2 slices stale bread
- Pure olive oil
- 2 cloves garlic, neatly cut
- Salt & pepper
- 2 small ripe of tomatoes or 6 cherry tomatoes, chopped
- ½ of a cucumber, sliced
- Capers
- ½ of red onion, neatly thinly cut
- Red wine vinegar
- ½ of bunch basil

Directions:

1. Cut the bread into bite-sized chunks.

2. Heat two tablespoons of pure olive oil in a griddle with the garlic and afterward add the bread and sauté until brown, blending regularly, until the bread absorbs the olive oil. Season with salt and eliminate the garlic.
3. Place the tomatoes, cucumber, and onion in a serving of mixed greens bowl with the tricks.
4. Blend a dressing in with two sections olive oil to one-section red wine vinegar, in addition to salt and pepper
5. Add the bread and dressing to the plate of mixed greens with the torn basil leaves. 6. Surrender to sit for to an hour to allow the bread to soft and the flavors to mix.

44. Pappa al pomodoro

PREPARATION TIME: 15 MINUTES SERVES 2

You will need:

- 2 tablespoons of pure olive oil, plus extra for serving
- 1 onion, neatly cut
- 2 cloves of garlic, neatly cut
- Pinch dried of chilli flakes
- 400g of can cut tomatoes
- 500 ml of water
- ½ of loaf stale bread, cut into pieces
- Salt & pepper
- ½ of bunch basil

Directions:

1. Heat the olive oil in a profound pan, then, at that point, sauté the onion, garlic, and chilli until softened.

2. Include the tomatoes and water and heat to the point of boiling, then, at that point, include the bread and keep on cooking, blending so often, until the bread has relaxed.
3. Include more water if important to get a soupy consistency.
4. Season to taste than not long prior to serving, mix in the basil leaves.
5. Garnish with a sprinkle of olive oil.

45. Old fashioned bread pudding

PREPARATION TIME: 30 MINUTES SERVES 4

You will need:

- 4 to 6 slices slightly stale bread
- 1 piece of fruit: apple, pear, peach, plum or nectarine
- 50g of any dried fruit e.g., mixed, sultanas, dates
- 50g of pure granulated sugar
- 1 egg
- 1 to 2 tablespoons of fruit juice
- 1 teaspoon of pure ground cinnamon
- 25g of any nuts
- ½ teaspoon of mixed spice
- 1 tablespoon of melted butter

Directions:

1. Preheat the oven to 200°C

2. Put the bread in a colander and softly wash with cold water.
3. Crush the bread dry with your hands or press with a spoon.
4. Place in a clean mixing bowl and squash in with a fork.
5. Strip and cut up the organic product into pieces.
6. Add new and dried organic products, blended zest, nuts, organic product squeeze, and egg to the bread and blend well.
7. Oil an ovenproof dish with softened margarine.
8. Move the combination to the dish and smooth utilizing the rear of a spoon.
9. Heat in the oven for around 45 minutes, until it turns golden and firm.

46. Eggy bread

PREPARATION TIME: 20 MINUTES SERVES 2

You will need:

- 4 slices of leftover bread
- 2 eggs, crack
- 2 tablespoons of milk Butter

Directions:

1. Combine the milk and eggs as one and fill a shallow dish.
2. Absorb the cuts of bread the egg combination, going to cover the two sides.
3. Heat the butter in a frying pot and, when softened, add however many cuts of the bread as you can fit in.
4. Fry tenderly on the two sides until browned.

47. Teatime bread and butter pudding

PREPARATION TIME: 30 MINUTES SERVES 2

You will need:

- 4 slices of slightly stale bread
- 50g of butter
- 25g of currants
- 25g of raisins
- 400ml of pure milk
- 5 to 6 used tea bags
- 4 large eggs
- 130g of light brown muscovado sugar
- 300ml of single cream
- 1 teaspoon of ground cinnamon
- 1 teaspoon of mixed spice

- 1 tablespoon demerara sugar

Directions:

1. Butter a 28x18cm, 5cm profound ovenproof dish.
2. Butter each cut of bread on one side and cut into four triangles.
3. Lay three cuts of bread (12 triangles) Butter side in the dish with the goal that they somewhat cross-over. Sprinkle over roughly ¾ of the currants and raisins.
4. Lay the leftover four triangles Butter side on top of different triangles and sprinkle with the excess currants and raisins.
5. Place the milk in a skillet with the tea packs. Stew for 15 minutes, blending at times until the tea has implanted the milk and turned it to a pale earthy colored tone. Include the cream, heat delicately for a further five minutes, and afterward eliminate the tea packs.
6. Break the eggs into a bowl, include the muscovado sugar, and speed until foamy. Presently empty the milk blend into the bowl of sugar and eggs. Include the cinnamon and blended flavor and rush until all fixings are consolidated.
7. Pour the fluid equitably over the bread triangles and sprinkle demerera sugar over the highest point of the bread.
8. Preheat the oven to 180°C (gas mark 4) then, at that point, heat for 30 minutes until set and brilliant.
9. Serve warm with cream or custard.

48. Banana berry yoghurt dessert

PREPARATION TIME: 10 MINUTES SERVES 2

You will need:

- 1 ripe banana neatly peeled, cut and frozen
- A handful of frozen berries
- 2 tablespoons of natural yoghurt
- Mint

Directions:

1. Mix together the frozen banana and frozen berries to make a smooth blend.
2. Include the yogurt and mix once more.
3. Serve garnished with a twig of mint and slashed fresh berries.
4. Eat straight or freeze in segments.

49. Banana bread

PREPARATION TIME: 15 MINUTES SERVES 8

You will need:

- 2 cups of pure flour
- ¾ of cup sugar
- 1 tablespoon of pure baking powder
- 1 teaspoon salt
- 2 eggs
- 3 medium-sized brown bananas
- 4 tablespoons of melted butter

Directions:

1. Cut and squeeze the bananas in a clean bowl and then include the eggs.
2. Mix in the dry ingredients & pour into greased tray
3. Bake at 180°C (gas mark 4) for one hour

50. Banana walnut muffins

PREPARATION TIME: 15 MINUTES MAKES 12 MUFFINS

You will need:

- 150ml of pure oil
- 100g of sugar
- 1 egg
- 2 bananas, squeeze
- 50g of walnuts, slice
- 200g of whole meal flour
- 50g of rolled oats
- 1 teaspoon of undiluted baking powder

Directions:

1. Pre-heat the oven stove to 180°C
2. In a clean bowl, blend the oil and sugar.

3. Include the egg and beat it well.
4. Blend in the banana and pecans.
5. Include the flour, oats, and baking powder and completely consolidate.
6. Set up a biscuit plate with 12 paper biscuit cases and separate the blend into the cases.
7. Prepare for 20 minutes and afterward cool on a wire rack

51. Smoothies

PREPARATION TIME: 5 MINUTES SERVES 4

You will need:

CLASSIC:

- 1 cup of strawberries
- 1 very ripe banana
- 2 tablespoons plain yoghurt
- 1 cup of orange juice

TROPICAL:

- 1 ripe mango
- 2 ripe bananas
- 1 cup plain yoghurt
- Juice of 1 lime

PEACH MELBA:

- 1 cup of raspberries
- 1 ripe banana
- 1 tin peaches in juice
- 1 cup of yoghurt

Directions:

1. Peel fruit & remove any pips or stones then sliced them into small pieces.
2. Mix all You will need: in a clean blender & blend until it is completely smooth.

52. Sorbet

PREPARATION TIME: 10 MINUTES SERVES 4

You will need:

- 300g of sugar
- 500ml of water
- Any ripe, soft fruit, puréed
- Juice of one lemon or lime

Directions:

1. Heat the sugar and water in a frying pan pot until the sugar has disintegrated.
2. Bring to the boil and afterward turn the hotness down and stew for five minutes.

3. When cool, add an equivalent amount of your natural product purée and lemon/lime juice.
4. Empty the sorbet into a glass or plastic dish and put it into the cooler.
5. Remove it from the freezer and beat it at regular intervals or thereabouts, until it is totally set.

53. Apple and pear cake

PREPARATION TIME: 25 MINUTES SERVES 4

You will need:

- 3 apples or pears
- Juice of ½ lemon
- 3 eggs, cracking
- 150g of brown sugar
- 90ml of vegetable oil
- 350g of undiluted flour
- 1-2 teaspoons of ground cinnamon or ginger
- 2 teaspoons baking powder

- Milk

Directions:

1. Preheat the oven to 180°C.
2. Softly oil a baking plate.
3. Cut the apples or pears and blend in a bowl with the lemon juice
4. In a bowl whisk together the eggs and the sugar until rich then, at that point, beat in the oil.
5. Sifter in the flour, cinnamon or ginger, and baking powder and blend.
6. Empty the mixture into the plate and arrange the fruit slices upright into the hitter to make an example.
7. Heat for 40 minutes until a stick embedded tells the truth.

54. Fruit crumble

PREPARATION TIME: 25 MINUTES SERVES 8

You will need:

- 1 bd of lemon juice
- 750g of pears
- Pinch ground cinnamon
- Pinch ground nutmeg
- 85g of golden caster sugar
- 85g of soft brown sugar
- 100g of plain flour
- 75g of margarine

- 75g of demerara sugar
- Pinch nutmeg

Directions:

1. Preheat the oven to 180°C
2. Oil a huge flan dish or cake tin.
3. Strip, core, and cut the natural product into little lumps and spot in a dish with the lemon juice.
4. Bring to the bubble and afterward stew tenderly.
5. Add the cinnamon, nutmeg, caster sugar, and delicate earthy colored sugar.
6. Cook, mixing every so often until delicate then spot into the flan dish.
7. In a different bowl, utilize your fingers or a fork to rub the flour and margarine together into pieces and afterward blend in the demerara sugar.
8. Scatter the crumble mix freely over the highest point of the natural product.
9. Heat for 20-30 minutes then, at that point, serve hot or cold.

55. Stewed apples

PREPARATION TIME: 10 MINUTES SERVES 4

You will need:

- 4 apples
- 1 tablespoon of water
- 20g of granulated sugar
- ½ teaspoon mixed spice
- 25g of sultanas

Directions:

1. Peel and core the apples and cut them into little pieces.
2. Place the apples in a pot with the water, sugar, and blended zest.
3. Cook over moderate heat, mixing periodically.
4. Following a couple of moments, the apple ought to be delicate. Add the sultanas and blend in, remove from the hotness.
5. Serve hot with frozen yogurt or cold with regular yogurt.

56. Steamed plum pudding

PREPARATION TIME: 25 MINUTES SERVES 6

You will need:

- 1 kg of plums, quartered & stoned
- 60g of caster sugar
- 175g of caster sugar
- 175g of butter, at room temperature
- 3 eggs
- 175g of self-rising flour

Directions:

1. Place the plums and 60g of caster sugar into a pot and cook for three to four minutes over medium heat.
2. Place 3/4 of this mix into a 1.2-liter pudding bowl.
3. For the wipe, place every one of the excess fixings into a bowl and rush for roughly three minutes, until light and soft.
4. Spoon this mix into the pudding bowl over the plums. Cover the bowl with greaseproof paper, got with string. Presently cover this with kitchen foil.
5. Place a heatproof saucer or little plate topsy turvy in the lower part of a huge skillet with a cover.
6. Place the pudding bowl onto the saucer then, at that point, empty water into the dish to come 66% the way up the side of the bowl.
7. Put the cover on the container and carry the water to the bubble. Lessen the hotness and steam for oneself and a half hour. Eliminate the bowl from the skillet. 8. Present with the excess plum blend, syrup, and custard or cream

57. Clementine cake

PREPARATION TIME: 30 MINUTES SERVES 12

You will need:

For the cake:

- 125g butter
- 175g of sugar
- 4 tablespoons of clementine juice
- 175g of pure self-rising flour
- 2 eggs

- Grated rind of
- 2 clementines

For the drizzle:

- 75g of icing sugar
- Juice of 2 clementines

Directions:

1. Put all the cake You will need: into a mixing bowl and blend until very much joined and you have a smooth batter.
2. Spoon into a loaf tin and heat at 180°C (gas mark 4) for around 45 minutes, until a stick confesses all and the highest point of the cake is golden.
3. Pour the icing and clementine juice into a pan and hotness delicately until the sugar has broken down.
4. At the point when the cake is cool, cautiously push the cake with a stick so there are a few openings and afterward shower with the syrup.

58. Orange preserve

PREPARATION TIME: 15 MINUTES This makes Two huge jars

You will need:

- 1kg of oranges
- 1.2kg of caster sugar
- 3 to 4 tablespoons of glucose
- 1 lemon juice
- 1 teaspoon of pure baking powder
- 1 glass of clean water

Directions:

1. Place the oranges in a clean frying pot, cover with water. Carry the water to the bubble and stew for five minutes, then, at that point, channel the oranges.
2. Repeat step one yet this time, add the baking powder.
3. In the case of utilizing entire oranges, cleave them into eight and eliminate the seeds and stem.
4. Add a layer of the orange parts of a container, cover with sugar and rehash this strategy until you have every one of your pieces in the skillet.
5. Add one major glass of water and bubble until the water is decreased considerably.
6. At this stage, there might be a meager layer of 'froth' on the outer layer of the dish. Provided that this is true, skim this off.
7. Add the glucose and lemon squeeze and leave it in the prospect hours.
8. The next day, bubble on low hotness again until the juice in the skillet has been decreased and it is transformed into a brilliant syrup.
9. At the point when the safeguard is prepared, scoop it into hot, dry, cleaned containers. Ensure every one of the orange pieces is covered with syrup and seal right away.

59. Red onion confit

PREPARATION TIME: 15 MINUTES MAKES 1 huge jar

You will need:

- 500g of red onions
- 2 tablespoons of pure olive oil
- 50g of demerara sugar
- 2 bay leaves
- 200ml of clen water
- 4 tablespoons of red wine vinegar
- Sterilized jar

Directions:

1. Halve & thinly cut the onions.
2. Heat the oil in a clean frying pan, then, at that point, tip in the onions and give them a decent mix so they are gleams with the oil.
3. Cook with the cover on for around 10 to 15 minutes, until they are truly soft and getting tacky on the lower part of the container. Be cautious as they can undoubtedly consume, yet the tacky pieces will be eliminated when you add the vinegar
4. Remove the lid, add the water, sugar, and vinegar and bring to the bubble.
5. The next step is to go down to a simmer and cook without the top for 45 - an hour until the onions are extremely delicate and the mixture is syrupy.
6. Taste and season as vital, then, at that point, fill a cleaned jar.

60. Spiced apple chutney

PREPARATION TIME: 25 MINUTES MAKES 3 JARS

You will need:

- 750g of cooking or other apples, peeled & diced
- 375g of light muscovado
- 250g of raisins
- 1 medium onion, neatly sliced
- 1 teaspoon of mustard seeds
- 1 teaspoon of pure ground ginger
- ½ teaspoon of salt
- 350ml of cider

- 3 sterilized jars

Directions:

1. Add all the You will need: in a clean, heavy saucepan.
2. Bring the mixture to a clean boil over a moderate or medium heat, then simmer uncovered, stirring frequently, for 30 to 40 minutes, or until thick & pulpy.
3. Remove from the heat, leave to cool & transfer to sterilized jars & seal.

61. Pumpkin marmalade

PREPARATION TIME: 45 MINUTES MAKES 4 JARS

You will need:

- 1 kg of pumpkin or squash
- 1750ml of clean water
- 1 orange, neatly cut into thin semi-circles
- 2 lemons, neatly cut into thin semi-circles
- 65g of fresh ginger root, finely shredded
- 750g of preserving
- 4 sterilized jars

Directions:

1. Strip the pumpkin and remove every one of the seeds and fibres
2. Cut the tissue into pieces and mesh lengthways, so the strands are as far as might be feasible.
3. Put the ground pumpkin in a pot with the water, oranges, lemons, and ginger. Bring to the bubble, then, at that point, stew for 25 - 30 minutes or until the citrus strip is simply delicate.
4. Include the sugar, mixing until it has disintegrated. Get back to the bubble, then, at that point, cook over medium hotness for 25 - 30 minutes or until the blend is thick enough for a wooden spoon attracted through the middle to leave an unmistakable channel.
5. Eliminate the frying pan from the heat and pass on the fruit to settle for a couple of moments. Scoop the marmalade into the hot sterilized containers and seal.

62. Kimchi

PREPARATION TIME: 30 MINUTES MAKES 2 huge jars

You will need:

- 1 head Chinese leaf/Napa cabbage, cut into 3cm chunks
- 1 daikon radish/mooli, gently cut into 1cm rounds
- 2 carrots, cut into 5cm long matchsticks
- 50g of fresh ginger, peeled & roughly chopped
- 5 cloves garlic, chopped
- 5 to 8 red chillies, de-seed
- 1 tablespoon of Asian Chilli pure powder

Brine:

- 6 tablespoons of sea salt
- 2 liters of clean water
- 2 sterilized jars

Directions:

1. Set up the brine by combining the water and salt, then, at that point, mix until the salt breaks down.
2. Add the pre-arranged vegetables. Put a plate or enormous plastic top on top and afterward a load on top, for example, a container loaded up with water. Permit this to splash for eight hours or short-term.
3. Remove the vegetables by scooping them out of the brackish water. Hold the brackish water for some time in the future.
4. Place the bean stew, bean stew powder ginger, and garlic in a food processor or blender and puree into the glue. Add brackish water depending on the situation to mix and make a thick glue.
5. Set on a couple of cleaning up or medical gloves so you don't consume your hands. Blend the glue into your vegetables well, being certain to cover each piece.
6. At long last, pack the kimchi into your pre-arranged containers. Try to leave a 3cm hole at the highest point of the container for the kimchi to grow.
7. Leave at room temperature for around four to eight days, checking the following four days for required 'harshness'.
8. At the point when the ideal flavor is reached, move the containers to the ice chest. This will save for quite a long time whenever kept refrigerated.

63. Simple courgette pickle

PREPARATION TIME: 20 MINUTES MAKES 1 huge jar

You will need:

- 2 small courgettes, neatly peeled, & cut into quarters or sixths lengthways
- 40g of salt per 1kg of courgettes
- Malt, cider or white wine
- 200ml of vinegar
- 1 teaspoon of honey to taste
- Spices
- 1 sterilized jar

Directions:

1. Toss courgettes and salt in a clean bowl and leave someplace cool for a considerable length of time. The salt will draw out an abundance of water, fundamental for the pickle to last.
2. In the meantime, carry a pan of vinegar to the bubble and improve it to taste with honey. You could add flavors as well.
3. Wash courgettes in a few changes of new water and channel well. Cautiously pack them into hot sanitized containers then, at that point, promptly pour over hot vinegar to cover.
4. Seal immediately. Store someplace cool and dim and they should most recent a year.

64. Sweet-sour lemons or limes

PREPARATION TIME: 15 MINUTES MAKES 2 jars

You will need:

- 8 unwaxed lemons
- 1 teaspoons of fine salt per lemon
- Sugar to taste
- Spices (optional, e.g., clove, pepper, cinnamon, bay, coriander)
- 2 sterilized jars

Directions:

1. Cut the majority of the fruit into four wedges.
2. Grind salt with flavors and add a little sugar to taste. Rub the blend all around the cut surfaces of the foods grown from the ground you truly do pack them into containers. Crunch them down to get the juices streaming.
3. Juice the leftover lemons/limes and top up the containers with this juice so that everything is shrouded in pungent citrus juice.
4. Close the container and leave someplace warm. If utilizing screw-top tops, close freely instead of fixing the top so gas can get away. They should begin bubbling inside seven days. Following a month, they should smell wonderfully matured and the skins will be delicate and prepared to utilize crude or cooked.
5. However long no form seems this safeguard will last indefinitely.

65. Watermelon rind jam

PREPARATION TIME: 20 MINUTES MAKES 1 jar

You will need:

- 500g of watermelon rind
- 200g of sugar
- Juice of 4 limes
- 1 sterilized jar

Directions:

1. Use a vegetable peeler to the outer dark green skin of the watermelon and dispose of it. Cleave the skin tissue into little pieces.
2. Blend the skin in a clean bowl with sugar and lime juice. Cover and leave for the time being.
3. The following day you should observe the sugar has taken out bunches of juice and broken up into it. Move the combination to an enormous pot and gradually heat to the point of boiling, guaranteeing any last sugar gems break down.
4. Bubble, mixing every so often, until the combination lessens to a jam-like consistency. This should take a little over 30 minutes.
5. Utilize a stick blender to mix the blend as smooth as you prefer, then, at that point, move to the disinfected container. Store in the fridge once opened.

66. Pumpkin chutney

PREPARATION TIME: 25 MINUTES MAKES 3 jars

You will need:

- 500g of pumpkin
- 2 onions
- 4 tablespoons of pure olive oil
- 75g of sugar

- 1 brambly apple
- 2 tomatoes
- 100g of sultanas
- 100ml cider vinegar
- ½ tablespoon of ground ginger
- ½ tablespoon of garam masala
- ½ teaspoon of chilli pure powder
- ½ tablespoon of dried thyme
- Salt & black pepper
- 3 sterilized jars

Directions:

1. Set the oven to 200oC.
2. Dice the pumpkin and put it on a cooking tin with a shower of olive oil and a sprinkle of salt. Cook on the stove for 30 minutes until relaxed and brilliant.
3. In the meantime, hack the onion and tomatoes into little 3D squares.
4. Heat two tablespoons of olive oil in an enormous weighty-based dish.
5. Add every one of the fixings aside from the vinegar and cook on low hotness.
6. At the point when the pumpkin is prepared, add to the container with the vinegar and cook for a further ½ hour or until the blend has thickened and is foaming gradually.
7. Season to taste, fill warm sterilized jars, and keep for four weeks to mature.

67. Vegetable end sauerkraut

PREPARATION TIME: 20 MINUTES MAKES 1 huge jar

You will need:

- 1 large red of cabbage
- Mix of vegetable ends (e.g., carrot tops or broccoli stalk)

- 15g of salt per 1kg vegetables
- 1 liter jar, sterilized

Directions:

1. Remove an outer leaf from the cabbage, wash well and put away.
2. Finely cut or mesh all the cabbage and vegetable finishes, then, at that point, gauge them.
3. Place the vegetables in an exceptionally huge bowl and sprinkle with 15g of salt per 1kg. Blend well and back rub unequivocally with two hands for a decent ten minutes until the vegetables are limp and have radiated a great deal of fluid.
4. Pack the vegetables and juice as firmly as conceivable into your sanitized container, leaving somewhere around a 5cm hole at the top to consider the juice to ascend as it matures. Utilize the cabbage leaf you put away before to cover the vegetables. The fluid necessities cover every one of the vegetables so air can't contact them. On the off chance that not add a little daintily salted water.
5. Close the container and leave it on top of a paper towel (on the off chance that it spills) at room temperature to age. Following a few days, you should begin to see little air pockets of gas ascending in the container. If utilizing a screw top you should 'burp' the sauerkraut every two or three days by opening then, at that point, resealing the top.
6. Smell and taste the sauerkraut following a multi-week. It should smell acrid, similar to sauerkraut. On the off chance that it tastes tart as you would prefer, it is prepared. In the event that not, continue maturing for one more little while.
7. When ready keep your sauerkraut in the ice chest to slow the aging and use throughout the following not many weeks as a plate of mixed greens.

68. Diet Jackal Fries

PREPARATION TIME: 10 MINUTES SERVES 2

You will need:

- 2 big eggs
- 1/2 cup ground Parmesan cheddar
- 1/2 cup toasted wheat germ
- 1 tablespoon Italian flavoring

- 3/4 tablespoon garlic salt
- 1 medium eggplant (around 1-1/4 pounds)
- Cooking splash
- 1 cup meatless pasta sauce, warmed

Directions:

1. Preheat Oven to 400°. In a shallow bowl, whisk eggs. In another shallow bowl, blend cheddar, wheat germ and seasonings.
2. Trim parts of the bargains; eggplant longwise into 1/2-in. - thick cuts. Cut cuts the long way into 1/2-in. strips. Plunge eggplant in eggs; at that point cover with cheddar blend.
3. Spritz eggplant and Atkins Diet bushel with cooking shower. Working in clumps, if necessary, place eggplant in a solitary layer in fryer crate and cook until brilliant darker, 5-7 Minutes. Turn eggplant; spritz with extra cooking splash. Keep cooking until brilliant dark colored, 4-5 Minutes. Serve promptly with pasta plunging sauce.

69. Spicy Hot Chicken

PREPARATION TIME: 40 MINUTES SERVES 6

You will need:

- 2 tablespoon dill pickle juice, separated
- 2 tablespoon hot pepper sauce, separated
- 1 tablespoon salt, separated

- 2 pounds chicken tenderloins
- 1 cup generally useful flour
- 1/2 tablespoon pepper
- 1 big egg
- 1/2 cup buttermilk
- Cooking splash
- 1/2 cup olive oil
- 2 tablespoon cayenne pepper
- 2 tablespoon dull dark colored sugar
- 1 tablespoon paprika
- 1 tablespoon stew powder
- 1/2 tablespoon garlic powder
- Dill pickle cuts

Directions:

1. In a bowl or shallow dish, consolidate 1 tablespoon pickle juice, 1 tablespoon hot sauce and 1/2 tablespoon salt. Add chicken and go to cover. Refrigerate, secured, at any rate 60 Minutes. Channel, disposing of any marinade. Preheat oven to 375°. In a shallow bowl, blend flour, staying 1/2 tablespoon salt and pepper. In another shallow bowl, whisk egg, buttermilk, staying 1 tablespoon pickle juice and 1 tablespoon hot sauce. Dunk chicken in flour to cover the two sides; shake off overabundance. Dunk in egg blend, on the other hand in flour blend.
2. In clumps, orchestrate chicken in a solitary layer in very much lubed Atkins Diet bin; spritz chicken with cooking shower. Cook until brilliant dark colored, 5-6 Minutes. Turn; spritz with cooking shower. Cook until brilliant dark colored, 5-6 Minutes longer. Whisk together cayenne pepper, dark colored sugar and seasonings; pour over hot chicken. Present with pickles.

70. Shrimp And mayonnaise dip

PREPARATION TIME: 35 MINUTES SERVES 4

You will need:

- 1/2 cup mayonnaise
- 1 tablespoon Creole mustard
- 1 tablespoon cleaved cornichons or dill pickles
- 1 tablespoon of shallot

- 1-1/2 tablespoons. lemon juice
- 1/8 tablespoon cayenne pepper

Directions:

1. For remoulade, in a little bowl, consolidate the initial 6 ingredients. Refrigerate, secured, until serving. Preheat Oven to 375°. In a shallow bowl, blend flour, herbs de Provence, ocean salt, garlic powder, pepper and cayenne. In a different shallow bowl, whisk egg, milk and hot pepper sauce. Spot coconut in a third shallow bowl. Dunk shrimp in flour to cover the two sides; shake off overabundance. Dunk in egg blend, at that point in coconut, tapping to help follow.
2. In clusters, master Minutes shrimp in a solitary layer in lubed Atkins Diet container; spritz with cooking splash. Cook until coconut is softly sautéed and shrimp turn pink, 3-4 Minutes on each side.
3. Spread cut side of buns with remoulade. Top with shrimp, lettuce and tomato.

71. Cheesy Egg Rolls Munch

PREPARATION TIME: 40 MINUTES SERVES 12

You will need:

- 1/2-pound mass pork wiener
- 1/2 cup destroyed sharp cheddar
- 1/2 cup destroyed Monterey Jack cheddar

- 1 tablespoon cleaved green onions
- 4 big eggs
- 1 tablespoon 2% milk
- 1/4 tablespoon salt
- 1/8 tablespoon pepper
- 1 tablespoon spread
- 12 egg move wrappers
- Maple syrup, discretionary

Directions:

1. In a little nonstick skillet, cook hotdog over medium warmth until never again pink, 4-6 Minutes, breaking into disintegrates; channel. Mix in cheeses and green onions; put in a safe spot. Wipe skillet clean.
2. In a little bowl, whisk eggs, milk, salt and pepper until mixed. In a similar skillet, heat margarine over medium warmth. Pour in egg blend; cook and mix until eggs are thickened and no liquid egg remains. Mix in wiener blend.
3. Preheat Oven to 400°. With one corner of an egg move wrapper confronting you, place 1/4 cup filling just underneath focus of wrapper.
4. In clumps, egg abounds in a solitary layer in lubed Atkins Diet bin; spritz with cooking splash. Cook until delicately seared, 3-4 Minutes. Turn; spritz with cooking splash. Cook until brilliant dark colored and fresh, 3-4 Minutes longer. Whenever wanted, present with maple syrup or salsa.

72. Tasty Chicken Tenders

PREPARATION TIME: 15 MINUTES SERVES 4

You will need:

- 1/2 cup panko (Japanese) bread pieces
- 1/2 cup potato sticks, squashed

- 1/2 cup squashed cheddar wafers
- 1/4 cup ground Parmesan cheddar
- 2 bacon strips, cooked and disintegrated
- 2 tablespoons. new chives
- 1/4 cup spread, softened
- 1 tablespoon sharp cream
- 1-pound chicken tenderloin

Directions:

1. Preheat Oven to 400°. In a shallow bowl, consolidate the initial six You will need. In another shallow bowl, whisk margarine and sharp cream. Plunge chicken in spread blend, at that point in morsel blend, tapping to help covering follow.
2. In bunches, orchestrate chicken in a solitary layer in lubed Atkins Diet bin; spritz with cooking shower. Cook until covering is brilliant dark colored and chicken is never again pink, 7-8 Minutes on each side. Present with extra harsh cream and chives.

73. Raspberry Balsamic Smoked Pork Chops

PREPARATION TIME: 15 MINUTES SERVES 4

You will need:

- 2 big eggs
- 1/4 cup 2% milk

- 1 cup panko (Japanese) bread scraps
- 1 cup finely cleaved walnuts
- 4 smoked bone-in pork cleaves (7-1/2 ounces each)
- 1/4 cup universally handy flour
- 1/3 cup balsamic vinegar
- 2 tablespoon darker sugar
- 2 tablespoon seedless raspberry jam
- 1 tablespoon defrosted solidified squeezed orange concentrate

Directions:

1. Preheat Oven to 400°. Spritz fryer container with cooking shower. In a shallow bowl, whisk together eggs and milk. In another shallow bowl, hurl bread pieces with walnuts.
2. Coat pork slashes with flour; shake off abundance. Dunk in egg blend, at that point in scrap blend, tapping to help follow. Working in clumps varying, place hacks in single layer in Atkins Diet crate; spritz with cooking shower.
3. Cook until brilliant darker, 12-15 Minutes, turning part of the way through cooking and spritzing with extra cooking splash. Evacuate and keep warm. Rehash with residual slashes. In the interim, place remaining You will need: in a little pot; heat to the point of boiling. Cook and mix until marginally thickened, 6-8 Minutes. Present with hacks.

74. Fritta Chicken

PREPARATION TIME: 35 MINUTES SERVES 6

You will need:

- Cooking splash
- 2 cups squashed Ritz wafers (around 50)

- 1 tablespoon of new parsley
- 1 tablespoon garlic salt
- 1 tablespoon paprika
- 1/2 tablespoon pepper
- 1/4 tablespoon ground
- 1/4 tablespoon scoured sage
- 1 enormous egg, beaten
- 1 grill/fryer chicken (3 to 4 pounds), cut up

Directions:

1. Preheat Oven to 375°. Spritz the fryer container with cooking splash.
2. In a shallow bowl, blend the following ingredients. Spot egg in a different shallow bowl. Plunge chicken in egg, at that point in wafer blend, tapping to help covering follow. Spot a couple of bits of chicken in a solitary layer in the readied crate, spritz with cooking shower.
3. Cook 10 Minutes. Turn chicken and spritz with extra cooking splash; cook until chicken is brilliant dark colored and squeezes run clear, 10-20 Minutes longer. Rehash with staying chicken.

75. Fish and Fries

PREPARATION TIME: 40 MINUTES SERVES 4

You will need:

- 1-pound potatoes (around 2 medium)
- 2 tablespoon olive oil

- 1/4 tablespoon pepper
- 1/4 tablespoon salt

Directions:

1. Preheat Oven to 400°. Strip and cut potatoes longwise into 1/2-in.- thick cuts; cut cuts into 1/2-in.- thick sticks.
2. In a big bowl, hurl potatoes with oil, pepper and salt. Working in clumps varying, place potatoes in a solitary layer in Atkins Diet bushel; cook until simply delicate, 5-10 Minutes Toss potatoes in bin to redistribute; keep on cooking until softly sautéed and fresh, 5-10 Minutes longer.
3. Meanwhile, in a shallow bowl, blend flour and pepper. In another shallow bowl, whisk egg with water. In a third bowl, hurl cornflakes with cheddar and cayenne. Sprinkle fish with salt; dunk into flour blend to cover the two sides; shake off abundance. Plunge in egg blend, at that point in cornflake blend, tapping to help covering follow.
4. Remove fries from crate; keep warm.
5. Place fish in a solitary layer in fryer crate. Cook until fish is daintily caramelized and simply starting to piece effectively with a fork, turning part of the way through cooking, 8-10 Minutes. Try not to overcook.
6. Return fries to bin to warm through. Serve right away.
7. If wanted, present with tartar sauce.

76. Diet Pickles

PREPARATION TIME: 20 MINUTES SERVES 4

You will need:

- 32 dill pickle cuts

- 1/2 cup universally handy flour
- 1/2 tablespoon salt
- 3 enormous eggs, softly beaten
- 2 tablespoon dill pickle juice
- 1/2 tablespoon cayenne pepper
- 1/2 tablespoon garlic powder
- 2 cups panko (Japanese) bread scraps
- 2 tablespoon cut crisp dill
- Cooking splash
- Ranch plate of mixed greens dressing, discretionary

Directions:

1. Preheat Oven to 400°. Let pickles remain on a paper towel until liquid is nearly ingested, around 15 Minutes.
2. Meanwhile, in a shallow bowl, consolidate flour and salt.
3. In another shallow bowl, whisk eggs, pickle juice, cayenne and garlic powder.
4. Combine panko and dill in a third shallow bowl.
5. Dip pickles in flour blend to cover the two sides; shake off abundance.
6. Dip in egg blend, at that point in scrap blend, tapping to help covering follow. Spritz pickles and fryer crate with cooking splash.
7. In groups, place pickles in a solitary layer in container and cook until brilliant darker and firm, 7-10 Minutes.
8. Turn pickles; spritz with extra cooking splash. Keep cooking until brilliant darker and fresh, 7-10 Minutes. Serve right away.
9. If wanted, present with farm dressing.

77. Apple Pie Egg Rolls

PREPARATION TIME: 15 MINUTES SERVES 8

You will need:

- 3 cups slashed stripped tart apples
- 1/2 cup pressed light dark colored sugar
- 2-1/2 tablespoons ground cinnamon, isolated

- 1 tablespoon corn starch
- 8 egg move wrappers
- 1/2 cup spreadable cream cheddar
- Butter-seasoned cooking splash
- 1 tablespoon sugar
- 2/3 cup hot caramel frozen yogurt besting

Directions:

1. Preheat Oven to 400°. In a little bowl, consolidate apples, dark colored sugar, 2 tablespoons cinnamon and corn starch.
2. With one corner of an egg move wrapper confronting you, spread 1 inadequate tablespoon cream cheddar to inside 1 in. of edges. Spot 1/3 cup apple blend just beneath focal point of wrapper.
3. (Cover remaining wrappers with a soggy paper towel until Preparation to utilize.)
4. Fold base corner over filling; soak remaining wrapper edges with water. Overlap side corners toward focus over filling. Move egg move up firmly, squeezing at tip to seal. Rehash.
5. In groups, orchestrate egg overflows with a solitary layer in lubed Atkins Diet container; spritz with cooking splash. Cook until brilliant darker, 5-6 Minutes. Turn; spritz with cooking splash. Cook brilliant dark colored and fresh, 5-6 Minutes longer. Join sugar and staying 1/2 tablespoon cinnamon; roll hot egg overflows with blend. Present with caramel sauce.

78. Garlic-Rosemary Brussels Sprouts

PREPARATION TIME: 30 MINUTES SERVES 4

You will need:

- 3 tablespoon olive oil
- 2 garlic cloves
- 1/2 tablespoon salt
- 1/4 tablespoon pepper
- 1-pound Brussels grows, cut and split

- 1/2 cup panko (Japanese) bread morsels
- 1-1/2 tablespoons crisp rosemary

Directions:

1. Preheat Oven to 350°. Spot initial 4 You will need: in a little microwave-safe bowl; microwave on high 30 seconds. Toss Brussels grows with 2 tablespoon oil blend. Spot all the Brussels grows in fryer container and cook 4-5 Minutes. Mix grows. Keep on airing fry until grows are daintily sautéed and close to wanted delicacy, around 8 Minutes longer, mixing part of the way through cooking time.
2. Toss bread pieces with rosemary and remaining oil blend; sprinkle over sprouts. Keep cooking until morsels are seared and grows are delicate, 3-5 Minutes. Serve right away.

79. Crab Cakes

PREPARATION TIME: 20 MINUTES SERVES 2

You will need:

- 1 medium sweet red pepper, finely cleaved
- 1 celery rib, finely cleaved
- 3 green onions, finely cleaved
- 2 enormous egg whites
- 3 tablespoon fat mayonnaise

- 1/4 tablespoon arranged wasabi
- 1/4 tablespoon salt
- 1/3 cup in addition to 1/2 cup dry bread scraps, partitioned
- 1-1/2 cups irregularity crabmeat, depleted cooking shower

Sauce:

- 1 celery rib, cleaved
- 1/3 cup fat mayonnaise
- 1 green onion, cleaved
- 1 tablespoon sweet pickle relish
- 1/2 tablespoon arranged wasabi
- 1/4 tablespoon celery salt

Directions:

1. Preheat Oven to 375°. Spritz fryer bin with cooking splash. Join initial 7 ingredients include 1/3 cup bread pieces. Tenderly overlap in crab.
2. Place remaining bread scraps in a shallow bowl. Drop stacking tablespoonful of crab blend into scraps. Tenderly coat and shape into 3/4-in. - thick patties. Working in groups varying, place crab cakes in a solitary layer in bushel. Spritz crab cakes with cooking shower.
3. Cook until brilliant dark colored, 8-12 Minutes, cautiously turning partially through cooking and spritzing with extra cooking splash. Expel and keep warm. Rehash with outstanding crab cakes.
4. Meanwhile, place sauce You will need: in nourishment processor; beat 2 or multiple times to mix or until wanted consistency is come to. Serve crab cakes promptly with plunging sauce.

80. Sweet and Sour Pineapple Pork

PREPARATION TIME: 15 MINUTES SERVES 4

You will need:

- 1 can (8 ounces) unsweetened squashed pineapple, undrained
- 1 cup juice vinegar
- 1/2 cup sugar
- 1/2 cup pressed dim dark colored sugar
- 1/2 cup ketchup
- 2 tablespoon sodium soy sauce

- 1 tablespoon Dijon mustard
- 1 tablespoon garlic powder
- 2 pork tenderloins (3/4 pound each), divided
- 1/4 tablespoon salt
- 1/4 tablespoon pepper
- Sliced green onions, discretionary

Directions:

1. In an enormous pan, consolidate the initial eight ingredients. Heat to the point of boiling; lessen heat. Stew, revealed, until thickened, 15-20 Minutes, blending every so often.
2. Preheat Oven to 350°. Sprinkle pork with salt and pepper. Spot pork in lubed Atkins Diet bin; spritz with cooking splash. Cook until pork starts to dark colored around edges, 7-8 Minutes. Turn; pour 1/4 cup sauce over pork. Cook until a thermometer embedded into pork peruses at any rate 145°, 10-12 Minutes longer. Let pork stand 5 Minutes before cutting. Present with outstanding sauce. Whenever wanted, top with cut green onions.

81. Coconut Shrimp and Apricot Sauce

PREPARATION TIME: 10 MINUTES SERVES 6

You will need:

- 1-1/2 pounds uncooked big shrimp
- 1-1/2 cups improved destroyed coconut
- 1/2 cup panko (Japanese) bread scraps
- 4 big egg whites
- 3 runs Louisiana-style hot sauce

- 1/4 tablespoon salt
- 1/4 tablespoon pepper
- 1/2 cup generally useful flour

Sauce:

- 1 cup apricot jelly
- 1 tablespoon juice vinegar
- 1/4 tablespoon squashed red pepper pieces

Directions:

1. Preheat Oven to 375°. Strip and devein shrimp, leaving tails on.
2. In a shallow bowl, hurl coconut with bread scraps. In another shallow bowl, whisk egg whites, hot sauce, salt and pepper. Spot flour in a third shallow bowl.
3. Dip shrimp in flour to cover gently; shake off abundance. Dunk in egg white blend, at that point in coconut blend, tapping to help covering follow.
4. Spray fryer container with cooking splash. Working in clumps varying, place shrimp in a solitary layer in bushel. Cook 4 Minutes; turn shrimp and keep cooking until coconut is delicately seared and shrimp turn pink, an additional 4 Minutes.
5. Meanwhile, join sauce You will need: in a little pot; cook and mix over medium-low warmth until jam are liquefied. Serve shrimp promptly with sauce.

82. Bourbon Bacon Cinnamon Rolls

PREPARATION TIME: 10 MINUTES SERVES 8

You will need:

- 8 bacon strips
- 3/4 cup whiskey
- 1 tube (12.4 ounces) refrigerated cinnamon moves with icing
- 1/2 cup slashed walnuts
- 2 tablespoon maple syrup

Directions:

1. Place bacon in a shallow dish; include whiskey. Seal and refrigerate medium-term. Evacuate bacon and pat dry; dispose of whiskey.
2. In an enormous skillet, cook bacon in bunches over medium warmth until about fresh yet flexible. Expel to paper towels to deplete. Dispose of everything except 1 tablespoon drippings.
3. Preheat Oven to 350°. Separate mixture into 8 moves, saving icing bundle. Unroll winding folds into long strips; pat batter to frame 6x1-in. strips. Spot 1 bacon strip on each piece of batter, cutting bacon varying; reroll, shaping a winding. Squeeze closures to seal. Rehash with outstanding batter. Move 4 moves to the Atkins Diet container; cook 5 Minutes. Turn turns over and cooks until brilliant dark colored, around 4 Minutes.
4. Meanwhile, join walnuts and maple syrup. In another bowl, mix ginger together with substance of icing bundle. In same skillet, heat remaining bacon drippings over medium warmth. Include walnut blend; cook, mixing frequently, until gently toasted, 2-3 Minutes.
5. Drizzle a large portion of the icing over warm cinnamon moves; top with a large portion of the walnuts. Rehash to make a subsequent cluster.

83. Fiesta Chicken Fingers

PREPARATION TIME: 25 MINUTES SERVES 4

You will need:

- 3/4-pound boneless skinless chicken bosoms
- 1/2 cup buttermilk
- 1/4 tablespoon pepper
- 1 cup universally handy flour
- 3 cups corn chips, squashed

- 1 envelope taco flavoring
- Sour cream farm plunge or salsa

Directions:

1. Preheat Oven to 400°. Pound chicken bosoms with a meat hammer to 1/2-in. thickness. Cut into 1-in. wide strips.
2. In a shallow bowl, whisk buttermilk and pepper. Spot flour in a different shallow bowl. Blend corn chips and taco flavoring in a third bowl. Plunge chicken in flour to cover the two sides; shake off overabundance. Plunge in buttermilk blend, at that point in corn chip blend, tapping to help covering follow. In clumps, chicken in a solitary layer in lubed Atkins Diet bushel; spritz with cooking shower. Cook until covering is brilliant dark colored and chicken is never again pink, 7-8 Minutes on each side. Rehash with staying chicken. Present with farm plunge or salsa.

84. Chocolate Chip Oatmeal Cookies

PREPARATION TIME: 10 MINUTES SERVES 6

You will need:

- 1 cup spread, mollified
- 3/4 cup sugar
- 3/4 cup stuffed dark colored sugar
- 2 big eggs

- 1 tablespoon vanilla concentrate
- 3 cups qquick-cooking oats
- 1-1/2 cups universally handy flour
- 1 bundle (3.4 ounces) moment vanilla pudding blend
- 1 tablespoon heating pop
- 1 tablespoon salt
- 2 cups (12 ounces) semisweet chocolate chips
- 1 cup slashed nuts

Directions:

1. Preheat Oven to 325°. In an enormous bowl, cream margarine and sugars until light and feathery. Beat in eggs and vanilla. In another bowl, whisk oats, flour, dry pudding blend, heating pop and salt; bit by bit beat into creamed blend. Mix in chocolate chips and nuts.
2. Drop mixture by tablespoonful onto heating sheets; smooth somewhat. In groups, place 1 in. separated in lubed Atkins Diet container. Cook until softly sautéed, 8-10 Minutes. Expel to wire racks to cool.

86. Chicken Strips

PREPARATION TIME: 15 MINUTES SERVES 4

You will need:

- 1 day-old everything bagel, torn
- 1/2 cup panko (Japanese) bread morsels
- 1/2 cup ground Parmesan cheddar
- 1/4 tablespoon squashed red pepper drops
- 1/4 cup margarine, cubed

- 1-pound chicken tenderloins
- 1/2 tablespoon salt

Directions:

1. Preheat Oven to 400°. Heartbeat torn bagel in a nourishment processor until coarse morsels structure. Spot 1/2 cup bagel scraps in a shallow bowl; hurl with panko, cheddar and pepper drops. (Dispose of or spare residual bagel scraps for another utilization.)
2. In a microwave-safe shallow bowl, microwave spread until dissolved. Sprinkle chicken with salt. Plunge in warm margarine, at that point cover with morsel blend, tapping to help follow. Shower Atkins Diet bushel with cooking splash. Spot chicken in a solitary layer in fryer bushel.
3. Working in bunches, if necessary, cook 7 Minutes; turn chicken over. Keep cooking until covering is brilliant dark colored and chicken is never again pink, 7-8 Minutes. Serve right away.

87. Green Tomato

PREPARATION TIME: 10 MINUTES SERVES 4

You will need:

- 2 medium green tomatoes (around 10 ounces)
- 1/2 tablespoon salt
- 1/4 tablespoon pepper
- 1 big egg, beaten
- 1/4 cup generally useful flour

- 1 cup panko bread pieces
- Cooking splash
- 1/2 cup decreased fat mayonnaise
- 2 green onions, finely hacked
- 1 tablespoon cut new dill or 1/4 tablespoon dill weed
- 8 cuts entire wheat bread, toasted
- 8 cooked focus cut bacon strips
- 4 Bibb or Boston lettuce leaves

Directions:

1. Preheat Oven to 350°. Cut tomato into 8 cuts, around 1/4 in. thick each. Sprinkle tomato cuts with salt and pepper. Spot egg, flour and bread pieces in isolated shallow dishes. Dunk tomato cuts in flour, shaking off abundance, at that point plunge into egg, lastly into bread piece blend, tapping to help follow.
2. In clumps, place tomato cuts in a solitary layer in lubed Atkins Diet bin; spritz with cooking splash. Cook until brilliant darker, 8-12 Minutes, turning midway and spritzing with extra cooking splash. Evacuate and keep warm.
3. Meanwhile, blend mayonnaise, green onions and dill. Layer every one of 4 cuts of bread with 2 bacon strips, 1 lettuce leaf and 2 tomato cuts. Spread mayonnaise blend over residual cuts of bread; place over top. Serve right away.

88. **Chicken Breasts**

PREPARATION TIME: 20 MINUTES SERVES 8

You will need:

- 2 cups buttermilk
- 2 tablespoon Dijon mustard
- 2 tablespoons salt
- 2 tablespoons hot pepper sauce
- 1-1/2 tablespoons garlic powder
- 8 bone-in chicken bosom parts, skin evacuated (8 ounces each)

- 2 cups delicate bread scraps
- 1 cup cornmeal
- 2 tablespoon canola oil
- 1/2 tablespoon poultry flavoring
- 1/2 tablespoon ground mustard
- 1/2 tablespoon paprika
- 1/2 tablespoon cayenne pepper
- 1/4 tablespoon dried oregano
- 1/4 tablespoon dried parsley pieces

Directions:

1. Preheat Oven to 375°. In an enormous bowl, consolidate the initial five ingredients. Add chicken and go to cover. Refrigerate, secured, 1 hour or medium-term.
2. Drain chicken, disposing of marinade. Join remaining You will need: in a shallow dish and mix to consolidate. Include chicken, each piece in turn, and go to cover. Spot in Atkins Diet crate showered with cooking splash in a solitary layer. Air fry until a thermometer peruses 170°, turning mostly, around 20 Minutes. Rehash with staying chicken. At the point when the last bunch of chicken is cooked, return all chicken to container and air fry 2-3 Minutes longer to warm through.

89. Cheese-Stuffed Burgers

PREPARATION TIME: 15 MINUTES SERVES 4

You will need:

- 2 green onions, daintily cut
- 2 tablespoon new parsley
- 4 tablespoons Dijon mustard, separated
- 3 tablespoon dry bread pieces
- 2 tablespoon ketchup
- 1/2 tablespoon salt

- 1/2 tablespoon dried rosemary, squashed
- 1/4 tablespoon dried sage leaves
- 1-pound lean ground meat (90% lean)
- 2 ounces cheddar, cut
- 4 burger buns, split
- Optional. Lettuce leaves, cut tomato, mayonnaise and extra ketchup

Directions:

1. Preheat Oven to 375°. In a little bowl, consolidate green onions, parsley and 2 tablespoons mustard. In another bowl, blend bread pieces, ketchup, seasonings and staying 2 tablespoons mustard. Add meat to bread piece blend; blend softly yet altogether.
2. Shape blend into 8 dainty patties. Spot cut cheddar in focus of 4 patties; spoon green onion blend over cheddar. Top with outstanding patties, squeezing edges together immovably, taking consideration to seal totally.
3. Place burgers in a solitary layer in Atkins Diet crate. Working in bunches varying, air-fry 8 Minutes; flip and keep cooking until a thermometer peruses 160°, 6-8 Minutes longer. Serve burgers on buns, with garnishes whenever wanted.

90. Lemon Slice Sugar Cookies

PREPARATION TIME: 25 MINUTES SERVES 8

You will need:

- 1/2 cup unsalted spread, mollified
- 1 bundle (3.4 ounces) moment lemon pudding blend
- 1/2 cup sugar
- 1 big egg, room temperature
- 2 tablespoon 2% milk

- 1-1/2 cups generally useful flour
- 1 tablespoon powder
- 1/4 tablespoon salt

Icing:

- 2/3 cup confectioners' sugar
- 2 to 4 tablespoons lemon juice

Directions:

1. In an enormous bowl, cream margarine, pudding blends and sugar until light and cushioned. Beat in egg and milk. In another bowl, whisk flour, Preparation powder and salt; continuously beat into creamed blend.
2. Divide mixture fifty-fifty. On a delicately floured surface, shape each into a 6-in.- long roll. Wrap and refrigerate 3 hours or until firm.
3. Preheat Oven to 325°. Unwrap and cut mixture transversely into 1/2-in. cuts. Spot cuts in a solitary layer in foil-lined fryer bushel. Cook until edges are light dark colored, 8-12 Minutes. Cool in bushel 2 Minutes. Expel to wire racks to cool totally. Rehash with outstanding mixture.
4. In a little bowl, blend confectioners' sugar and enough lemon juice to arrive at a sprinkling consistency. Shower over treats. Let remain until set.
5. Wrap and spot in a resalable compartment. Store in the fridge.
6. Freeze choice: Place enveloped logs by a resalable compartment and freeze. To utilize, unwrap solidified logs and cut into cuts. Cook as coordinated, expanding time by 1-2 Minutes.

91. Pepper Minutest Lava Cakes

PREPARATION TIME: 30 MINUTES SERVES 4

You will need:

- 2/3 cup semisweet chocolate chips
- 1/2 cup spread, cubed
- 1 cup confectioners' sugar
- 2 big eggs
- 2 big egg yolks
- 1 tablespoon pepper Minutest remove

- 6 tablespoon generally useful flour
- 2 tablespoon finely squashed pepper Minutest confections, discretionary

Directions:

1. Preheat Oven to 375°. In a microwave-safe bowl, liquefy chocolate chips and spread for 30 seconds; mix until smooth. Rush in confectioners' sugar, eggs, and egg yolks and concentrate until mixed. Overlay in flour.
2. Generously oil and flour four 4-oz. ramekins; empty hitter into ramekins. Try not to overload. Spot ramekins in fryer bin; cook until a thermometer peruses 160° and edges of cakes are set, 10-12 Minutes. Try not to overcook.
3. Remove from broiler; let stand 5 Minutes. Deliberately run a blade around sides of ramekins a few times to slacken cake; reverse onto dessert plates. Sprinkle with squashed confections. Serve right away.

92. Sweet Potato Tots

PREPARATION TIME: 20 MINUTES SERVES 4

You will need:

- 2 little (14 oz. absolute) sweet potatoes,
- peeled 1 tablespoon potato starch
- 1/8 tablespoon garlic powder
- 1/4 tablespoons genuine salt,
- divided 3/4 cup no-salt-included ketchup cooking splash

Directions:

1. Heat a medium pot of water to the point of boiling over high warmth. Include potatoes, and cook until simply fork delicate, around 15 Minutes. Move potatoes to a plate to cool, around 15 Minutes.
2. Working over a medium bowl, grind potatoes utilizing the big gaps of a case grater. Tenderly hurl with potato starch, garlic powder and 1 tablespoon salt. Shape blend into around 24 (1-inch) tot-molded chambers.
3. Daintily cover Atkins Diet crate with cooking splash. Spot 1/2 of tots (around 12) in single layer in the bushel, and splash with cooking shower. Cook at 400°F until gently sautéed, 12 to 14 Minutes, turning tots' part of the way through cook time. Expel from fry bushel and sprinkle with 1/8 tablespoon salt. Rehash with outstanding tots and salt. Serve promptly with ketchup.

93. Diet Doughnuts

PREPARATION TIME: 35 MINUTES SERVES 8

You will need:

- 1/4 cup warm water, warmed (100F to 110F)
- 1 tablespoon dynamic dry yeast 1/4 cup, in addition to
- 1/2 tsp. granulated sugar,
- divided 2 cups (around 8 1/2 oz.) universally handy flour

- 1/4 tablespoon genuine salt 1/4 cup entire milk, at room temperature 2 tablespoon unsalted spread, dissolved 1 big egg, beaten 1 cup (around 4 oz.) powdered sugar 4 tablespoons faucet water

Directions:

1. Mix together water, yeast, and 1/2 tablespoon of the granulated sugar in a little bowl; let remain until frothy, around 5 Minutes. Join flour, salt, and staying 1/4 cup granulated sugar in a medium bowl. Include yeast blend, milk, margarine, and egg; mix with a wooden spoon until a delicate batter meets up. Turn mixture out onto a daintily floured surface and work until smooth, 1 to 2 Minutes. Move batter to a softly lubed bowl. Spread and let ascend in a warm spot until multiplied in volume, around 60 Minutes.
2. Turn batter out onto a gently floured surface. Tenderly move to 1/4-inch thickness. Cut out 8 doughnuts utilizing a 3-inch round shaper and a 1-inch round shaper to evacuate focus. Spot doughnuts and doughnuts gaps on a gently floured surface. Spread freely with saran wrap and let remain until multiplied in volume, around 30 Minutes.
3. Spot 2 doughnuts and 2 doughnuts openings in single layer in Atkins Diet bushel, and cook at 350°F until brilliant dark colored, 4 to 5 Minutes. Rehash with outstanding doughnuts and gaps.
4. Whisk together powdered sugar and faucet water in a medium bowl until smooth. Dunk doughnuts and donut openings in coat; place on a wire rack set over a rimmed heating sheet to permit abundance coating to trickle off. Let remain until coat solidifies, around 10 Minutes.

94. Avocado Fries

PREPARATION TIME: 14 MINUTES SERVES 4

You will need:

- 1/2 cup (around 2 1/8 oz.) generally useful flour
- 1 1/2 tablespoons dark pepper
- 2 big eggs 1 tablespoon water
- 1/2 cup panko (Japanese-style breadcrumbs)
- 2 avocados, cut into 8 wedges each cooking splash

- 1/4 tablespoon legitimate salt
- 1/4 cup no-salt-included ketchup
- 2 tablespoon canola mayonnaise
- 1 tablespoon apple juice vinegar
- 1 tablespoon Sriracha stew sauce

Directions:

1. Mix together flour and pepper in a shallow dish. Delicately beat eggs and water in a subsequent shallow dish. Spot panko in a third shallow dish. Dig avocado wedges in flour, shaking off overabundance. Dunk in egg blend, permitting any overabundance to dribble off. Dig in panko, squeezing to follow. Coat avocado wedges well with cooking splash.
2. Spot avocado wedges in Atkins Diet container, and cook at 400°F until brilliant, 7 to 8 Minutes, turning avocado wedges over part of the way through cooking. Expel from Atkins Diet; sprinkle with salt.
3. While avocado wedges cook, whisk together ketchup, mayonnaise, vinegar, and Sriracha in a little bowl. To serve, place 4 avocado fries on each plate with 2 tablespoon sauce

95. Churros with Chocolate Sauce

PREPARATION TIME: 1 Hour 25 MINUTES SERVES 12

You will need:

- 1/2 cup water
- 1/4 tablespoon genuine salt
- 1/4 cup, in addition to
- 2 Tablespoon. unsalted spread, isolated

- 1/2 cup (around 2 1/8 oz.) generally useful flour
- 2 big eggs
- 1/3 cup granulated sugar
- 2 tablespoons ground cinnamon
- 4 ounces ambivalent heating chocolate, finely cleaved
- 3 tablespoon overwhelm cream
- 2 tablespoon vanilla kefir

Directions:

1. Bring water, salt, and 1/4 cup of the margarine to a bubble in a little pot over medium-high. Decrease warmth to medium-low; include flour, and mix energetically with a wooden spoon until mixture is smooth, around 30 seconds.
2. Mix together sugar and cinnamon in a medium bowl. Brush cooked churros with staying 2 tablespoon liquefied margarine, and move in sugar blend to cover.
3. Spot chocolate and cream in a little microwavable bowl, microwave on HIGH until liquefied and smooth, around 30 seconds, blending following 15 seconds. Mix in kefir. Serve churros with chocolate sauce.

96. Catfish with Green Beans

PREPARATION TIME: 25 MINUTES SERVES 2

You will need:

- 12 ounces crisp green beans cut cooking shower
- 1 tablespoon light darker sugar
- 1/2 tablespoon squashed red pepper (discretionary)

- 3/8 tablespoon fit salt, partitioned
- 2 Unit (6-oz.) catfish filets
- 1/4 cup universally handy flour
- 1 enormous egg, gently beaten
- 1/3 cup panko (Japanese-style breadcrumbs)
- 1/4 tablespoon dark pepper
- 2 tablespoon mayonnaise
- 1 1/2 tablespoons finely slashed crisp dill
- 3/4 tablespoon dill pickle relish
- 1/2 tablespoon apple juice vinegar
- 1/8 tablespoon granulated sugar Lemon wedges

Directions:

1. Spot green beans in a medium bowl, and splash generously with cooking shower. Sprinkle with dark colored sugar, squashed red pepper (if utilizing), and 1/8 tablespoon of the salt. Spot in Oven, and cook at 400°F until all around caramelized and delicate, around 12 Minutes.
2. In the interim, hurl catfish in flour to cover, shaking overabundance from fish. Plunge pieces, 1 at once, in egg to cover, at that point sprinkle with panko, squeezing to cover uniformly on all sides.
3. Fish in Atkins Diet bin; splash with cooking shower. Cook at 400°F until caramelized and cooked through, around 8 Minutes. Sprinkle best equitably with pepper and staying 1/4 tablespoon salt.
4. While fish is cooking, whisk together mayonnaise, dill, relish, vinegar, and sugar in a little bowl. Serve fish and green beans with tartar sauce and lemon wedges.

97. loaded baked potatoes

PREPARATION TIME: 25 MINUTES SERVES 2

You will need:

- 11 ounces child Yukon Gold potatoes (around 8 [2-inch] potatoes)
- 1 tablespoon olive oil
- 2 focus cut bacon cuts
- 1 1/2 tablespoon hacked crisp chives
- 1/2 ounce finely destroyed decreased fat cheddar (around 2 Tablespoon.)
- 2 tablespoon decreased fat sharp cream

- 1/8 tablespoon legitimate salt

Directions:

1. Hurl potatoes with oil to cover. Spot potatoes in Oven bushel, and cook at 350°F until fork delicate, 25 Minutes, mixing potatoes infrequently.
2. In the interim, cook bacon in a medium skillet over medium until firm, around 7 Minutes. Expel bacon from container; disintegrate. Spot potatoes on a serving platter; softly pound potatoes to part. Sprinkle with bacon drippings. Top with chives, cheddar, harsh cream, salt, and disintegrated bacon

98. Roasted Salmon

PREPARATION TIME: 50 MINUTES SERVES 4

You will need:

- 2 tablespoons finely cleaved new level leaf parsley
- 1 tablespoon finely cleaved new thyme
- 1 tablespoon genuine salt, partitioned
- 4 (6-oz.) skinless focus cut salmon filets
- 2 tablespoon olive oil

- 4 cups meagerly cut fennel (from 2 [15-oz.] heads fennel)
- 2/3 cup 2% decreased fat Greek yogurt
- 1 garlic clove, ground
- 2 tablespoon new squeezed orange (from 1 orange)
- 1 tablespoon new lemon juice (from 1 lemon) 2 tablespoon cleaved crisp dill

Directions:

1. Preheat Oven to 200°F.
2. Mix together parsley, thyme, and 1/2 tablespoon of the salt in a little bowl. Brush salmon with oil; sprinkle equitably with herb blend.
3. Spot 2 salmon filets in Atkins Diet container, and cook at 350°F until wanted level of doneness, 10 Minutes. Move to preheated stove to keep warm. Rehash system with outstanding filets.
4. While salmon cooks, hurl together fennel, yogurt, garlic, squeezed orange, lemon juice, dill, and staying 1/2 tablespoon salt in a medium bowl. Serve salmon filets over fennel plate of mixed greens.

99. Peach Hand Pie

PREPARATION TIME: 1 hour-20 MINUTES SERVES 8

You will need:

- 2 (5-oz.) crisp peaches, stripped and hacked
- 1 tablespoon crisp lemon juice (from 1 lemon)
- 3 tablespoon granulated sugar
- 1 tablespoon vanilla concentrate

- 1/4 tablespoon table salt
- 1 tablespoon cornstarch
- 1 (14.1-oz.) pkg. refrigerated piecrusts Cooking shower

Directions:

1. Mix together peaches, lemon juice, sugar, vanilla, and salt an in medium bowl. Let stand 15 Minutes, blending every so often. Channel peaches, holding 1 tablespoon liquid. Whisk cornstarch into held liquid; mix into depleted peaches.
2. Cut piecrusts into 8 (4-inch) circles. Spot around 1 tablespoon filling in focus of each circle. Brush edges of mixture with water; overlap batter over filling to frame half-moons. Pleat edges with a fork to seal; cut 3 little cuts in top of pies. Coat pies well with cooking shower.
3. Spot 3 pies in single layer in Atkins Diet container, and cook at 350°F until brilliant darker, 12 to 14 Minutes. Rehash with residual pies.

100. Diet Calzones

PREPARATION TIME: 42 MINUTES SERVES 7

You will need:

- 1 tablespoon olive oil
- 1/4 cup finely cleaved red onion (from 1 little onion)
- 3 ounces infant spinach leaves (around 3 cups)
- 1/3 cup lower-sodium marinara sauce

- 2 ounces destroyed rotisserie chicken bosom (around 1/3 cup)
- 6 ounces crisp arranged entire wheat pizza batter
- 1 1/2 ounces pre-destroyed part-skim mozzarella cheddar (around 6 Tablespoon.)
- Cooking shower

Directions:

1. Warmth oil in a medium nonstick skillet over medium-high. Include onion, and cook, blending infrequently, until delicate, 2 Minutes. Include spinach; spread and cook until shriveled, 1/2 Minutes. Expel skillet from heat; mix in marinara sauce and chicken.
2. Gap mixture into 4 equal pieces. Roll each piece on a gently floured surface into a 6-inch circle. Spot one-fourth of the spinach blend over portion of every mixture circle. Top each with one-fourth of the cheddar. Overlap batter over filling to shape half-moons, creasing edges to seal. Coat calzones well with cooking splash.
3. Spot calzones in Oven, and cook at 325°F until mixture is brilliant dark colored, 12 Minutes, turning calzones over following 8 Minutes.

101. Chicken and sweetcorn soup

PREPARATION TIME: 42 MINUTES SERVES 4

You will need:

- 1 tablespoon of pure vegetable oil
- 1 medium onion, sliced

- 1 level teaspoon of pure bouillon powder
- 1 medium potato, sliced
- 200g of cooked chicken, sliced
- 200g of frozen sweetcorn
- 1 teaspoon of dried mixed herbs
- 500ml of clean water
- 500ml of semi-skimmed milk

Directions:

1. Heat the oil in an enormous dish and fry the diced onion with the bouillon powder for a couple of moments, mixing constantly, until the onion mellow
2. Include all the other recipes: aside from the milk, bring to the bubble, and stew for around 15 - 20 minutes.
3. Include the milk and y re-heat.

102. Easy minestrone soup

PREPARATION TIME: 12 MINUTES SERVES 5

You will need:

- 50g of small pasta pieces

- 500g of carton of passata
- 350g of frozen mixed vegetables
- 2 tablespoons of pure vegetable oil
- 1 teaspoon of bouillon powder
- 1 teaspoon of dried mixed herbs
- 800ml of water

Directions:

1. Include all the above recipes to a big frying pan.
2. Bring down to the boil stirring to avoid the pasta sticking to the bottom.
3. Reduce the heat & simmer for about 20 minutes until the pasta is perfectly cooked.
4. Mix well before serving

103. Leek, potato and pea soup

PREPARATION TIME: 22 MINUTES SERVES 4

You will need:

- 11/2 tablespoons of pure vegetable oil

- 2 to 3 large leeks, clean and sliced
- 2 large of potatoes, clean and sliced
- 400ml of water
- 1 teaspoon of pure bouillon powder
- 1 teaspoon of dried mixed herbs
- 600ml of semi-skimmed milk
- 200g of frozen peas

Directions:

1. Heat the oil in a huge container, include the leeks and potatoes, and cook for around 5 minutes.
2. Include the water, bouillon powder, and spices, and stew until the vegetables are delicate.
3. Include the milk and peas and hotness through until the peas are cooked.
4. Sieve, squash, or mix the soup

104. Lentil and carrot soup

PREPARATION TIME:28 MINUTES SERVES 6

You will need:

- 2 tablespoons of vegetable oil
- 1 teaspoon of garlic paste
- 1 teaspoon of bouillon powder
- 3 to 4 large carrots, peeled and sliced
- 165g of dried red lentils
- 1 liter of water (1,000ml)

Directions:

1. Heat the oil in a clean frying bot, including the garlic, bouillon powder, and carrots, and fry tenderly, mixing routinely, for 5 minutes.
2. Include the lentils and water and bring to the bubble, mixing sometimes.
3. Stew for around 20 minutes until the lentils are delicate.
4. Either serve the soup all things considered, with pieces, or squash, sifter, or mix to make a smooth soup or on the other hand if serving it to a child.

105. Jacket potato with beef stir-fry T

PREPARATION TIME: 52 MINUTES SERVES 4

You will need:

- 4 large of jacket potatoes

For the filling:

- 11/2 tablespoons of vegetable oil
- 1 large onion, peeled and sliced
- 200g of lean beef, cut into strips
- 1 big carrot, peeled and sliced
- 1 large of courgette, clean, topped & tailed & sliced
- 1 red of pepper, seeds removed and sliced
- 3 tablespoons of soy sauce

Directions:

1. Heat the oil in an enormous dish, including the cut onion and hamburger strips, and fry, blending constantly, until the meat is seared.
2. Include the carrot, courgette, red pepper, and stir-fry over high hotness until the vegetables are mellowing and the meat is cooked.
3. Include the soy sauce and blend well
4. Serve the stir-fry over the cooked coat potatoes.

106. Jacket potato with scrambled egg and spinach

PREPARATION TIME: 52 MINUTES SERVES 7

You will need:

- 4 large of jacket potatoes, cooked
- For the filling:
- 25g of vegetable fat spread
- 250g of frozen spinach
- 5 large of eggs, cracked

Directions:

1. Melt the fat spread in a frying bot, include the frozen spinach, and cook until thawed out and relaxed.
2. Include the beaten eggs and cook, blending continually, until the eggs and spinach are blended and the egg is cooked.
3. Serve quickly on the cooked coat potatoes.

107. Jacket potato with tuna, sweetcorn and soft cheese

PREPARATION TIME: 120 MINUTES SERVES 4

You will need:

- 4 large of jacket potatoes, cooked
- 200g of frozen sweetcorn
- 1 can of tuna fish in brine
- 200g low-fat soft cheese
- 3 or 4 of spring onions, sliced

Directions:

1. Place the sweetcorn in boiling water, bring to the boil, & then drain and rinse.
2. Mix all the ingredients together in a bowl and serve immediately over hot cooked jacket potatoes

108. Jacket potato with vegetable chilli

PREPARATION TIME: 25 MINUTES SERVES 4

You will need:

- 4 large of jacket potatoes, cooked
- 11/2 tablespoons of pure vegetable oil
- 1 small of onion, sliced
- 1 teaspoon of pure bouillon powder
- 1 red pepper, seed remove and sliced
- 2 big tomatoes, sliced
- 1 big can (400g) red kidney beans
- 1 teaspoon of chilli powder
- 1 teaspoon of dried mixed herbs

Directions:

1. Heat the oil in a clean frying bot, include the diced onions and bouillon powder, and fry, blending constantly, until the onions mellow.
2. Include the wide range of various fixings and stew delicately, blending routinely, for around 10 minutes until every one of the vegetables is delicate.
3. Serve over cooked coat potatoes.

109. Baked bean and veggie sausage hotpot

PREPARATION TIME: 42 MINUTES SERVES 8

You will need:

- 11/2 tablespoons of pure vegetable oil
- 1 small onion, sliced
- 1 teaspoon of garlic paste
- 1 large of potato, washed & sliced
- 4 carrots, peeled & sliced
- 4 vegetarian sausages, each must be cut into 4 to 5 pieces
- 1 large can (400g) sliced tomatoes
- 1 large can (400g) reduced-salt, reduced-sugar baked beans
- 200g of frozen peas
- 350ml of clean water

Directions:

1. Heat the oil in a clean frying bot and fry the onion and garlic until the onion begins to relax.
2. Include all the other ingredients to the frying bot and mix well.
3. Bring to the boil and simmer gently for around 16 minutes until the vegetables are cooked.

110. Creamy chicken and leek hotpot

PREPARATION TIME: 90 MINUTES SERVES 4

You will need:

- 2 tablespoons of pure vegetable oil
- 2 large leeks, sliced into 1cm slices
- 3 big carrots, peeled & sliced
- 2 to 3 stalks celery, washed & sliced
- 300g of chicken breasts, sliced
- 400g of potatoes, sliced
- 100g of frozen green beans, sliced
- 500ml of pure water
- 200g of low-fat soft cheese

Directions:

1. Heat the oil in an enormous skillet. Include the leeks, carrots, celery, and chicken and fry for 2 to 3 minutes.
2. Include the potatoes, green beans, and water, bring to the boil, and stew for around 20 minutes until the vegetables and chicken are cooked.
3. Switch off the heat, mix in the soft cheddar until equitably disseminated, and serve right away.

111. Goulash

PREPARATION TIME: 52 MINUTES SERVES 4

You will need:

- 11/2 tablespoons of pure vegetable oil
- 1 small onion, sliced
- 350g of lean pork meat, sliced
- 1 green pepper, seed must be remove & cut
- 1 large of potato, sliced
- 2 large (400g) cans chopped tomatoes
- 1 large (400g) can cannellini beans drained & rinsed
- 1 tablespoon of pure paprika powder
- 1 teaspoon of pure bouillon powder
- 1 teaspoon of dried mixed herbs

Directions:

1. Heat the vegetable oil in a frying bot and fry the onion and pork until the meat is browned on all sides and the onion is beginning to relax.
2. Include the green pepper and potato and fry for 1 or 2 minutes.
3. Include the wide range of various recipes brought to the bubble and afterward stew for 15 to 20 minutes until every one of the recipes is cooked.

112. Egg-fried rice

PREPARATION TIME: 42 MINUTES SERVES 4

You will need:

- 400ml of water
- 200g of white rice
- 6 big eggs
- 2 tablespoons of pure vegetable oil
- 3 to 4 spring onions, sliced
- 1 red pepper, seed must be removed

Directions:

1. Carry the water to the boil, including the rice, bring to the boil again and mix once. Put a top on the skillet and stew for around 5 to 10 minutes. Switch off the hotness and leave the rice in the skillet with the top. It ought to retain all the water and be delicate.
2. Break the eggs into a bowl and beat them until the yolks and whites are blended.
3. In a griddle, heat the oil and fry the onion and red pepper until they mellow.
4. Include the rice in the vegetables and heat through.
5. Pour the egg combination over the rice and, mixing constantly, cook the blend until the eggs are cooked.
6. Serve immediately

113. Jerk chicken with rice and beans

PREPARATION TIME: 48 MINUTES SERVES 8

You will need:

- 1 big skinless chicken breast sliced
- 1 heaped of tablespoon jerk seasoning
- 1 tablespoon of pure vegetable oil
- 1 small onion, sliced
- 1 green pepper, the seed must be remove & sliced
- 1 large can red kidney beans, drained & rinsed
- 200g of white rice
- 400ml of clean water

Directions:

1. Coat the chicken fingers in jerk preparing and mix well. Leave in the ice chest for an hour to marinate.
2. In a clean frying bot, heat the oil and fry the onion and green pepper for 2 to 3 minutes.
3. Include the chicken and cook for 2 to 3 minutes.
4. Include the kidney beans, rice, and water in the combination and bring to the bubble.
5. Simmer for around 20 minutes with the top on the skillet until the rice has absorbed the water and the chicken and vegetables are cooked.

114. Turkey and vegetable pilaf

PREPARATION TIME: 12 MINUTES SERVES 4

You will need:

- 2 tablespoons of pure vegetable oil
- 1 teaspoon of garlic paste
- 1 teaspoon of dried mixed herbs
- 1 teaspoon of pure bouillon powder
- 200g of raw turkey breast, sliced
- 1 green pepper, seed must be removed and sliced
- 1 big of tomato, sliced
- 150g of frozen sweetcorn
- 200g of white rice
- 400ml of clean water

Directions:

1. Heat the oil in a clean frying bot and include the garlic, spices, bouillon powder, and turkey strips.
2. Cook for a couple of moments, stirring occasionally until the turkey is somewhat browned.
3. Include the vegetables and rice and cook tenderly for 1 moment.
4. Pour over the water, bring to the bubble mixing constantly and afterward stew tenderly for around 15 minutes with a cover on until the rice and vegetables are cooked.

115. Vegetable biryani

PREPARATION TIME: 78 MINUTES SERVES 4

You will need:

- 2 tablespoons of pre vegetable oil
- 2 tablespoons of medium pure curry powder
- 1 teaspoon of pure bouillon powder
- 1 onion, sliced
- 1 big carrot, peeled & sliced
- 1 big potato, sliced
- 100g of frozen peas
- 1/2 cauliflower, sliced
- 1 big can (400g) chickpeas, drained & rinsed
- 200g of white rice
- 400ml of clean water

Directions:

1. Heat the oil in a clean frying bot include the curry powder, bouillon powder, and onion and cook for a few minutes until the onion softens.
2. Include the carrot, potato, peas, cauliflower, chickpeas, and rice and stir for 1 minute.
3. Pour over the water and simmer gently with the lid on the pan for about 20 minutes until the rice is tender and the vegetables are all cooked.

116. Green mac and cheese

PREPARATION TIME: 25 MINUTES SERVES 5

You will need

- 500g of macaroni
- 1 head broccoli, cut into florets
- 200g of low-fat soft cheese
- 200ml of semi-skimmed milk

Directions:

1. Cook the macaroni in bubbling water for around 15 minutes until it is delicate. After the initial 10 minutes, place the broccoli in the same frying bot as the macaroni, or steam it over the bubbling macaroni in a colander.
2. Drain the macaroni and broccoli and afterward mix in the low-fat delicate cheddar and milk.
3. Heat through if important, before serving.

117. Pasta with green beans and peas

PREPARATION TIME: 27 MINUTES SERVES 5

You will need:

- 450g of dry pasta
- 2 tablespoons of pure vegetable oil
- 1 small onion, sliced
- 1 teaspoon of pure bouillon powder
- 250g of frozen green beans
- 250g of frozen broad beans
- 300g of frozen peas

Directions:

1. Cook the pasta or spaghetti in bubbling water until cooked and then drain.
2. In a huge dish, heat the oil and fry the onion and bouillon powder for a couple of moments until the onion is soft.
3. Include the leftover vegetables and hotness through with a cover on until the vegetables are cooked.
4. Blend the pasta and vegetable combination together and serve.

118. Spaghetti Bolognese

PREPARATION TIME: 52 MINUTES SERVES 2

You will need:

- 200g of lean minced beef
- 1 small onion, sliced
- 1 medium carrot, peeled & grated
- 1 teaspoon of garlic purée
- 1 teaspoon of bouillon powder
- 1 teaspoon of dried mixed herbs
- 1 big can sliced tomatoes
- 75g of porridge oats
- 200ml of clean water
- 450g of spaghetti

Directions:

1. Dry-fry the mince with the onion, carrot, garlic, bouillon powder, and blended spices until the mince is browned.
2. Include the tomatoes, oats, and water and stew delicately for 15 to 20 minutes with a cover on until the meat and vegetables are cooked.
3. While the Bolognese is cooking, heat up the spaghetti in water until delicate, and afterward channel.
4. Serve the Bolognese sauce over the pasta.

119. Tuna pasta

PREPARATION TIME: 12 MINUTES SERVES 6

You will need:

- 450g of dried pasta
- 2 tablespoons of pure vegetable oil
- 1 small onion, sliced
- 1 green pepper, seed must be remove & sliced
- 1 teaspoon of garlic paste
- 1 teaspoon of dried mixed herbs
- 1 teaspoon of pure bouillon powder
- 11/2 big cans (400g) sliced tomatoes
- 2 cans tuna in brine, drained

Directions:

1. Heat up the dried pasta in an enormous skillet of water until it is cooked.
2. Heat the oil in a frying bot and include the onion, pepper, garlic, spices and bouillon powder and fry, blending consistently, until the onions and peppers are delicate.
3. Include the canned tomatoes and fish and hotness through.
4. Include the cooked pasta and mix completely until the fish pasta is warmed through.

120. Peanut butter & banana sandwiches, with carrot & cucumber

PREPARATION TIME: 30 MINUTES SERVES 2

You will need:

- 8 slices whole-meal bread
- 4 tablespoons of peanut butter
- 2 big bananas, sliced
- 2 big carrots, peeled & sliced
- 1/2 of cucumber, clean & sliced

Directions:

1. Spread the peanut butter onto four cuts of the bread.
2. Include the cut banana and top each sandwich with one more cut of bread.
3. Serve the sandwiches with carrot and cucumber sticks.

121. Pitta bread with houmous and cucumber, with carrot salad

PREPARATION TIME: 24 MINUTES SERVES 2

You will need:

- 4 whole-meal pitta bread
- 300g of houmous
- 120g of cucumber, sliced
- 3 big carrots sliced
- 60g of raisins
- 11/2 tablespoons of pure vegetable oil

Directions:

1. Toast the pitta bread, & then cut off one end of each pitta to let out the steam & make a pocket.
2. Fill with houmous & cucumber.
3. Mix the grated carrot, raisins and oil to make a salad.

122. Savoury couscous salad with tuna

PREPARATION TIME: 42 MINUTES SERVES 5

You will need:

- 300g of couscous
- 200g of frozen sweetcorn
- 550ml of boiling clean water
- 1 can tuna in brine
- 100g of cherry tomatoes sliced
- 1 big can chickpeas, drained & rinsed
- 11/2 tablespoons of pure vegetable oil
- 1 tablespoon of sliced herbs (parsley, mint or coriander)

Directions:

1. Put the couscous and frozen sweetcorn in an enormous bowl.
2. Pour the bubbling water over it, mix and leave to assimilate all the water. Cushion with a fork when cool.
3. Drain the fish and piece the fish.
4. Include the chipped fish and the wide range of various fixings to the couscous, stirring well.

123. Apple crumble

PREPARATION TIME: 49 MINUTES SERVES 4

You will need:

- 65g of white flour
- 50g of vegetable fat spread
- 65g of porridge oats
- 40g of sugar
- 5 eating apples
- 1 teaspoon of mixed spice or cinnamon powder

Directions:

1. Heat the oven to 180°C/350°F/Gas 4.
2. Put the flour in a bowl and add the fat spread to it. Rub the fat spread into the flour with your fingertips until it takes after breadcrumbs.
3. Add the porridge oats and sugar and combine them as one.
4. Strip and cut the apples.
5. Put the apples into a heatproof baking dish, add the zest or cinnamon and combine as one.
6. Place the crumble mixes over the apple and put the disintegrate in the broiler for 30 to 35 minutes until the natural product is delicate and the crumble browned.

124. Banana custard

PREPARATION TIME: 22 MINUTES SERVES 2

You will need:

- 30g of custard powder
- 500ml of semi-skimmed milk
- 30g of sugar
- 4 big bananas

Directions:

1. Mix 1 or 2 tablespoons of the milk with the custard powder to make paste.
2. Put the excess milk in a pan to warm. Before it comes to the bubble, add the custard combination gradually, mixing constantly so it mixes in and doesn't go uneven, and afterward add the sugar.
3. Mix the custard well as it comes to the bubble and afterward stew for a couple of moments until it thickens.
4. Strip the bananas and cut them into lumps.
5. Place in a bowl and add the custard.

125. Poached pear with Greek yoghurt and honey

PREPARATION TIME: 56 MINUTES SERVES 2

You will need:

- 4 big pears
- 4 tablespoons of honey
- 360g of Greek yoghurt

Directions:

1. Peel the pears, remove the core and cut into quarters.
2. Place the pears in a pan of tenderly stewing water and poach for around 15 minutes.
3. Eliminate the poached pears and spot them in a serving bowl.
4. Sprinkle with honey and present with Greek yogurt.

CONCLUSION

In conclusion, to consider is the healthful and nutritional component part of the recipe. It doesn't imply that all recipes contain the same number of vitamins and minerals. Most of these recipes are tried and tested. I, personally have my home running on these recipes. My visitors think that I actually order food from outside. I could not get a better compliment than this and I simply smile back at them!

Printed in Great Britain
by Amazon

20690802R00093